Getting to Nantucket

Getting to *Nantucket*

AN ARTIST'S JOURNEY

Kerry Hallam

WITH JEFF MOSES

CORINTHIAN
BOOKS

Mt. Pleasant, S.C.

Publisher's Cataloging-in-Publication
(Provided by Quality Books, Inc.)

Hallam, Kerry.
　　Getting to Nantucket : an artist's journey / by
Kerry Hallam, with Jeff Moses - 1st ed
　　p. cm.
　　LCCN: 00-100886　　ISBN: 1-929175-05-1

　　1. Hallam, Kerry. 2. Painters – United States –
Biography. I. Moses, Jeff (Jeffrey) II. Title

ND237.H25A4 2000　　　　　　　759.13 [B]
　　　　　　　　　　　　　　QB100-180

Corinthian Books
an imprint of
the Côté Literary Group
P.O. Box 1898
Mt. Pleasant S. C. 29465-1898
(843) 881-6080
http://www.corinthianbooks.com

In recognition of an artist's journey:

Ruth Moses, an integral part of this journey, one of the very
few real artists I have known
Jeff, for his mammoth contribution to this book
Roy, who, like all good friends, remains
a complete enigma
David and Eric, who I have not yet managed to exhaust
David Alexander, the closest thing I will have to a brother
Freddy, my friend, who counts
Jack, for his focus
Wayne, who miraculously captured my music
from those distant golden years
D3
My Mother, departed now, but always with me
My Father, long gone, who carved our names on a tree in
Westwood one fine Spring morning
To the many friends and colleagues, for being there when I
needed them

For Karyad

In most cases, this portion of the book would be reserved for a precis of the author's life; where he was born and why; where he spent his early days and what it is that makes him instantly acceptable as a candidate for family talk shows on TV.

This is a little different. Most of that kind of information you will find in the book, should you choose to read it.

I served in Her Majesty's Armed Forces attached to the Gurkha Brigade. It was two years of the most hilarious tomfoolery you could imagine. I had a wonderful time, thanks to the incongruity of the Army's bureaucratic machinery and I had the good fortune to live in such exotic places as Hong Kong, Singapore, and Northern Malaysia. At that time, they were still loosely attached to the British Commonwealth. I was stationed there long enough to see, firsthand, a sample of the many reasons why this is no longer the case. All in all an enriching if somewhat jaundiced experience to which anyone who has been through that particular mill will testify.

This book begins about three years after I returned to the U.K. and drags you, panting and in need of a drink, up to the present time. Currently, I live and work on Nantucket Island. I earn my daily bread and a reasonable bottle of Vin Rouge every now and then through my painting. My art publishers sell what I produce, bless their cotton socks.

My guitar languishes in its case in the corner of my study. Every once in a while, I take it out, just to show that I still care. My fingers are not what they once were though, and my callouses are gone. But I am quite content in my little cottage. It suits my needs at this time.

My daughter Karyad is now age ten, going on forty. I see her about once every month. She seems to be doing just fine, and I marvel at her exquisite soul, her delightful inquisitive mind, and the sheer wonder and magic that she finds in ordinary day to day living. Of course I love her deeply, but also, and perhaps more importantly, I like her.

Having reached an age that I thought I would never see, I am amused to find that I am expected to be wise. I suppose the rationale is that anyone that has lasted this long doing what I do must have some kind of answer. I wish this were the case, but it isn't. I am capable of making the same rash decisions and silly mistakes as when I was a spotty teenager with pubescent thoughts and unhealthy appetites.

But for those who find themselves traveling the rather rocky road of creative expression, I have a few thoughts.

Society in general does not take kindly to creative people. We are a constant threat. We seek truth and enlightenment – dangerous stuff for most people. Disturbing stuff. Be prepared to be prepared. There is no such thing as overnight success. It usually takes about ten to fifteen years of very hard work. The strong survive and get to do what they want to do; say what they want to say; go where they want to go and, with luck, take a few of us with them. It takes grit, determination, and unshakable commitment or a very large trust account. Better still if you are lucky enough to have both.

The weak will fall by the wayside.

Which is just as well, really. The fewer vehicles there are on the road, the less chance there is of a bottleneck.

Enjoy the book.

Kerry Hallam
Nantucket Island
February 2000

1

London Transition

In the early 1960s old granny London kicked back her heels, took an extra swig from the cider barrel, and tossed her knickers in the air. Life was a carousel that never stopped spinning. Don't trust anyone over thirty and heave the old out the window.

It was a time of excessive excess. The abuse to which we subjected our poor bodies would have put normal people in the hospital. But then, we weren't normal! We had a keen awareness that we were living in a remarkable time and felt compelled to make as much of it as we could.

All good things come to an end though. 'Round about the early 70s, Swinging London had a nervous breakdown. The party finally ended with no one there to pick up the empty glasses and get the deposits back on the bottles.

Our vision in those splendiferous days didn't reach to the distant hills. We were happy with that over-accommodating playground. And who wouldn't have been? The Arts were in the forefront of the new wave. Artists were both the cheerleaders and the people being cheered — an exhilarating state of affairs. I don't think any of us knew why this was so, and we didn't particularly care. We simply enjoyed the release and dutifully led the procession. And what a procession it was!

Abstract Expressionism at the Whitechapel.
Beyond the Fringe.
Look Back in Anger.

Film, theatre, literature, art. London's creative houses, sitting with curtains drawn, were awakened from a dark sleep.

It suited us down to the ground. We relished it, twirled it around, danced with it, and took it to bed. The riotous, raucous, roaring band played on and on. It was strong liquor, frothy and seductive. One never seemed to drive to work in the morning from the same direction. We all agreed that we were on one hell of a ride.

But in the still quiet hours, the beginning of an irksome little notion disturbed me now and again. It didn't slow things down or get in the way. It just popped up unexpectedly. A thin, small voice would nudge me, whispering, "Take a look at yourself, young man. What do you see? Where are you going? And the work you do. What does it provide other than a brown envelope every Friday?"

Then, the even more disturbing questions, "Are you making the most of your artistic talent? When you're an old man sitting by the fire, will you look back at these days as wasted time? When, when, when will you truly begin to become an artist?"

I would take stock of these disturbing thoughts, go slightly out of balance, stop drinking and smoking for a couple days, then forget about them altogether and proceed on just as I had. After all, I didn't have it so bad. I certainly wasn't making full use of my college art education, but I did work as a designer in one of London's leading advertising agencies. As long as I showed up sober and on time, and was able to continue presenting the illusion of competence and enthusiasm, my position would continue, albeit at a pittance.

I drove a nifty light-blue Austin Mini Cooper with a leather-wrapped steering wheel. This beauty was capable of impressive turns of speed. I shared a comfortable maisonette with two close friends in fashionable Kensington. My social life, not to mention my love life, was full to overflowing.

To what then did I owe this malcontent? I decided to talk things over with my flatmates.

They thought perhaps I simply needed a bit of change and advised an immediate holiday on the continent. This was completely out of my financial scope, but the advice was offered in the right spirit.

Perhaps change of a different sort?

There is no greater procrastinator than a man of reduced means. However, having aired my concerns, my inner dissatisfaction took on greater importance. Once you open problems to scrutiny, they demand solution.

I had reason, I suppose, to be concerned. Much of my childhood and my entire university experience focussed on the pursuit of art as a career. After the death of my father, when I was thirteen, my mother and I were in continual financial distress. Although indecently young, I arranged to sell a watercolour here and there through a local merchant. The idea of being paid for something that until then had been a childhood pastime was heady wine.

I recall the brisk crackling winter morning when I wove my way through the bustling country market, passing greengrocer stalls ripe with the smells of fresh celery and brussel sprouts, the fruiter with oranges and bananas in hanging bunches, women's clothing stalls, shoe stalls, corset stalls — all jostling with business. Entire place settings for half price. Imagine.

Mr. Alf, a chubby, chortling fellow with long mutton chops and an old Derby hat, was winding up an old gramophone. I had been assured that he was always interested in unusual items for his stall. Clearing my throat to get his attention, I walked right up to him.

"Mr. Alf, I have a watercolour I did the other day. I've put it in a frame and I think it looks really nice. Are you interested?"

He surveyed my masterpiece. "I don't reckon there's a business fa watter culurs or whatever ya call um."

"Tell you what, Mr. Alf. You show the watercolour on your stall for the day. If it sells, you pay me half. If not, I'll take it home at five-thirty."

Such is the temerity of the destitute.

"Well," he said, scrunching his face around and scratching

his mutton chops, "won't cost owt to try, I reckon. And what do we know we might 'ave a buddin' Rembrandt on our hands!" He launched into a cackling laugh, then shouted to a passing housewife, telling her how much she would be missing if she didn't buy one of his used tea kettles. I returned at four o'clock. I could wait no longer. Sure enough, it was gone! Alf dropped five tinkling shillings in my hand and gave me a hearty slap on the back. I never asked how much he sold it for or who bought it.

On reflection, if any single event in my young life stirred my dormant creative soul, it was the moment I received money for that little watercolour. When I scurried home to show my mother the shining coins, I was thrilled beyond reckoning.

I wish I could tell you that I was a child prodigy, but my artistic origins were much more pragmatic. Art appealed to my basic instinct of larceny.

I wanted to produce more stuff to sell at Saturday market so Mum and I could buy an extra sausage or two for dinner or yarn for a new sweater in winter. If it meant more watercolours of the "Lake District in Spring," that was just fine by me.

My singular quest for income became stymied by the close attention that my art teacher was beginning to give me. I made the unspeakable mistake of asking if he could suggest efficient ways to double my output and raise my prices. It was the only time I ever saw him lose his temper.

"It's not so much that I mind you making a couple of extra shillings at the weekend," he said a few days later after calming down, "but I've every hope that you have what it takes to become a real artist. I mean a real one. A person of vision and integrity, capable of creating significant works of substance and importance. Not some hack that paints whatever the current popular subject happens to be."

Soon after, Alf took ill and retired from trade. Fate had saved me from further artistic degradation.

My art teacher set about grooming me with ferocious intensity. All my free time was to be spent drawing plaster anatomical molds. Invariably, Friday afternoons found me lugging home a plaster cast of a hand or foot, from which I was expected to produce half a dozen studies by Monday.

It would be impossible to put a value on the months spent in that unrelenting curriculum. Unquestionably they later helped me gain the much coveted admission and scholarship to the Art College in London. That which I regarded as a punishment turned out to be a blessing.

Yet there I was, nearly a decade later, employed in a London advertising agency. Rather than paints and brushes, my tools were straightedge and mechanical pencil. My imagination was continually circumscribed by deadlines and budgets.

Reflecting on my lot, I realized that I was quite a distance from the goals that my art instructor had envisioned for me. My existence was rather silly, consisting of a banal routine that produced nothing by week's end. No person had ever been given an Order of the British Empire or a laurel wreath for industrial design.

Most of my friends were involved in the arts in some form. They were writers, actors, painters. None had achieved the pinnacle of success yet, but they were giving it a go.

Of even greater concern, the frantic life in London seemed to have gained the better of me. What was to be accomplished, ultimately, by the delirious turmoil? What had I achieved? Where was I headed?

As is often the case, fate had my problem well in hand. The agency presented me a sizable project. I was to be responsible for the design and installation of a large trade show exhibit for an illustrious client. Conveniently putting aside all inner doubts about the value of my work and the life I had been living, I planned to design an exhibit of sufficient quality to submit to the Society of Industrial Designers in support of my application for membership.

I laboured over the concept, spending hours of overtime refining the intricate electrical, plumbing, and construction details. I wanted every element to be perfect, from the artistic to the practical. It was a gigantic job, even by agency standards. The completed working drawings and visual layouts formed a thick sheaf of over fifty pages.

The final bids arrived, and to the delight of my supervisor, I had brought the job in twenty-five percent under estimate. This news would be well received by his fellow directors, he assured me.

By that time I was confident that my design warranted an architectural award and would automatically place me among the industrial design immortals. Not to be overlooked was the raise and bonus that would be forthcoming for simply being a genius.

The one ticklish problem I'd had throughout the design process was working with the obnoxious account executive overseeing the project. He was responsible for feeding me data from all departments involved, so I could coordinate the many details into the overall design.

From the outset, this man had been a pain. He was arrogant and opinionated, constantly overbearing and oppressive. For him, the artistry of a design and even its ultimate functionality were of no consequence. His acknowledged corporate responsibility was to keep things on schedule, but it was apparent at all times that his only real interest was to cover his own butt.

On more than one occasion I had been obliged to bite my tongue in his presence, taking comfort in the conviction that my reward would soon come in tangible form. Most of the time, I was able to keep my focus on the important thing: my design. But I often entertained visions of embedding my T-square deeply into the crown of his pompous head.

Finally, after weeks of intense night-and-day activity, everything was ready for commencement of construction. I had completed final plans, and agreed upon strategies with all the contractors involved, had signed off on all final changes, and had given approval for the ordering of materials. Most of the prefabricated sections had already been manufactured, so we would have a little breathing room at the end of the project.

Two days before construction was to begin, Mr. Congeniality himself burst into my studio to alert me about extensive changes that he wanted made. I remained calm, explaining that it would be difficult to change even the slightest detail because all materials had been ordered and much of the construction already completed.

"Now, Kerry," he said, nose in the air and arse tight as a tick's, "there's no way out of this. The clients want these changes made, and that's that."

"Sorry," I said, "there's nothing I can do. You're too late." I finally was wielding a little power.

"Looks like I'll have a word with your boss, then." He was not going to die gracefully.

I returned to my drawing board, confident that artistic truth and my supervisor's eternal fanaticism about staying under budget would win the day.

A few minutes later, Mr. Congeniality returned with my supervisor, Mr. Pinstripe. There followed long minutes of huffing and puffing, much cigar smoke blown in my direction, some marginal, insincere compliments of my work, and devious, darting glances between them.

"Let's put it this way," my supervisor said to me, finally getting to it, "looks like you'll be working at home this weekend. Got to make these changes."

Mr. Congeniality was having a fine old time. He could not have squeezed another ounce of smugness out of his half smile.

I made one last try.

"Sir, with all due respect, I've worked the last four weekends on this project. Any revisions at this stage will mean major changes for the contractors, which will make it hard to stay on budget. Anyway, I really don't see any advantage . . . ."

I was interrupted by another stream of smoke.

"Hallam, make the bloody changes, or I will. Get my drift?"

The two retired to the inner sanctum of Mr. Pinstripe's office. Through the glass door I watched them continue to discuss the job, glancing every now and then in my direction.

I fixed my gaze on the distant rooftops. Late afternoon sunlight was catching the top of St. Paul's, casting the spires and steeples in a brilliant orange-red. The rumble of rush hour traffic from the street below floated up and through my open window. Not only had I lost the battle, but another weekend.

The meeting in my supervisor's office broke up. He strolled over to my drafting table.

"You're a good designer, Hallam. Stick to that and leave the politics to us. I'll see if I can squeeze a few extra hours out of accounts for you at the end of the month."

With that, he turned and left for the weekend.

I was revolted with myself. Not only would I have to perform a monumental selling job on the contractors, severely compromising my design in the process, I knew that I should have stood my ground. My self-esteem had taken a bad knock.

I sulked and brooded for an hour or so, then decided to call it a day and work at home over the weekend. Sheafing through the working drawings in my supervisor's office to sort out what I needed to take with me, I noticed a roll of drawings under the table. Glancing through them, I saw immediately that they were a complete set of my sketches for the project. Included were drawings and spec sheets from A to Z. At the bottom of each sheet was written "Designed Exclusively By" with my supervisor's name. Included with the drawings was his application for his own membership in the Society of Industrial Designers.

2

Putney Common Crossroads

I t took about two hours to gather every blueprint, drawing, layout, and scrap of paper that had any connection with the job. It was a sizeable bundle, and I worried that someone would stop me on the way out. I blew ten bob and took a taxi home.

That evening at a local pub I told my flatmates what had happened. We were on our second pint, and I was still seething.

"It's unfair," they agreed. "It's savage and criminal and anti-Art and contrary to all that's creative and worthwhile in the world. What the hell? Get used to it. That's life."

Standing up, I told them I needed some fresh air.

Strolling alone across Putney Common, I was deep in thought. It had been a long, trying day. Early that morning, as I had rushed to catch the Tube to work, I could not have imagined that by late afternoon my "suit-and-tie, Yes-Sir-No-Sir, three-bags-full" job would be completely awash.

I was most certainly at the crossroads I had been anticipating.

My anger began to subside, and in its place developed the germ of an idea. Continuing to walk across the common and along the footpath by the Thames, I became determined to use this opportunity to change, to make a life for myself of which I could be proud.

More of a life, less of the doldrums.

The question was how to begin my transformation. I had no money to fall back on. The meagre weekly wage on which I had been existing did not allow the luxury of saving. More often than not, by Wednesday I was borrowing food money.

I wasn't married. Not even vaguely attached. My love life had been decidedly active, but walking alone that night and looking at past months with the clarity that so often accompanies major change, my relationships with women seemed for the most part a sham. Full of bravado, with no substance. I had very willingly joined the hunt and run with the pack, giving little thought to anything more than finding a willing companion for the evening.

No ties or encumbrances in that area.

Wind whistled across the common, bringing the scent of approaching snow. I pulled my overcoat across my chest. Something was going to change. I felt that I had already made a start.

Throwing all caution known to mankind straight into the face of the freezing wind, I decided to leave England and head to southern France. There I would become the painter I knew was inside me. There I would meet my destiny. There I would find, at least, some warmth in the breeze.

The longing to live in a warm, or even tropical, climate had a deep origin. Born in Stavely, a bleak, perpetually frigid little town a hundred or so miles north of London, I had dreamed of greenery and balm most of my life.

Stavely. The very word induces a crouching in my soul. If ever a town exemplified the worst of northern industrial England, it was Stavely. In the first half of the twentieth century, it was a foul, phlegmatic place. Every nook and cranny was coated with a layer of black soot from the steel mills, acid manufacturing plants, engineering works, and collieries.

For the vast majority of Her Majesty's citizenry, even today there is hardly ever a reason to stop at Stavely. It's always a place on the way to somewhere else. The innumerable pubs soaked in beer and the odd grocery or gentlemen's outfitters with ten-year old grey suits in the window underscore the fact that Stavely has no humor at all. The town never smiles. It creaks at the seams with rheumatics and a bad cough. Stavely is where I began. My childhood spent in its sulfuric haze of shaded greys and blacks made a permanent impression. I have been impelled since then toward color and clarity, toward brightness and the sun's warmth.

Walking that freezing Friday evening through Putney Common, snow approaching, the thought of starting afresh in southern France was irresistible. By Sunday evening I had sublet my part of the maisonette. My flatmates thought I was potty, but they accepted my decision with good grace and severe doubts. I sold my few remaining goods and shackles at various pawn shops, and by Monday evening had raised the princely sum of sixty pounds. Trading in my spiffy blue mini for a dilapidated but more practical bright orange minivan, I at least would be clearly visible on the road — a plus when driving among the French. I packed my few remaining possessions, and on a hard cold morning with snow beginning to settle on streets and sidewalks, I said goodbye to London and motored off.

In the back of the van was the roll of drawings and designs for the exhibition booth. To this day I'm not sure if the booth was ever built. I'd like to think that it wasn't.

3

Ferry to France

I leaned on the stern railing of the British Railways channel ferry, watching the White Cliffs of Dover fade to grey and slip into the coastal mist. A thin veil of sunshine tried to break through, with no real enthusiasm. My spirits were high nonetheless, and I watched with a born-again artist's eye the ferry ponderously slosh and bump through the whitecaps, trailing a frothing wake above which gulls dived in a cackling ballet.

Our engines throbbed and shuddered as we pitched in the heavy sea. I went into the lounge and downed a hearty English breakfast of bacon and eggs, bangers and beans, and stewed tomatoes, padding it with two mugs of sweet tea. As I ate, the dishes slid back and forth across the table to the tilting of the ship.

At the ferry's *Bureau de Change* I exchanged my pound notes for a bundle of French currency, which was much more convenient. For one thing, it was on the decimal system. One hundred centimes to the Franc was a damn sight easier to work with than 240 pennies to the pound.

England at that time had an alarming array of coins and notes. Coins consisted of farthings, half-pennies, three-penny pieces, sixpences, shillings, two shilling pieces and half-crowns.

Paper money was somewhat simpler, consisting of ten shilling, one pound, and five pound notes. I think there were also ten and twenty pound notes, but I had never seen nor owned one. Trouser pockets were not made to house this mass of coinage and folding paper. The French system was lighter on the pockets and simpler to figure.

Clutching the bundle of paper bills with elaborately engraved French heroes in blues and pinks and filigree patterns, I stocked up at the duty-free shop. A bottle of cognac, a few chocolate bars and a carton of cigarettes − your basic emergency rations.

The crossing had been a bit lumpy, but we were reasonably on time as we pulled into the harbor at Calais. I went below and inched my orange van out through customs and passport control. I slid past the stone-faced excise man and finally arrived on French soil, remembering to drive on the wrong side of the road.

France was oblivious to my arrival. The inhabitants showed no sign of acknowledging that this was a most memorable day. It hardly mattered. Nothing could have dampened my euphoria. I was going to savor the moment. Wrap it up and keep it in a box beneath the bed. Every now and then I'd take it out and have a good chortle.

For the ordinary was extraordinary.

Everywhere about me were houses, French houses, made of French bricks. Even the French colours were different. Louvered lattice windows were like stonewashed cotton permeated with faded greens, lapis blues, and Venetian reds. Walls of houses faced higgledy-piggledy with sunbleached coats of paint. Cockeyed chimney pots brooded in terra cotta. Wrought iron rusting, random railings, and balconies sang a different song, a French song.

The architecture appeared haphazard and eccentric, but utterly charming and distinctive. Everything had been designed, manufactured, and built by a completely different mentality.

The road was jammed with cars that made peculiarly French noises. Signs over the shops glowed and twinkled. Catchy French phrases popped up on billboards with radiant French faces.

All French.

All very, very French.

A friend was living in Paris, so I set off along Rt. 43 for Arras which, according to the map and complex road signs, would take me to the N-1 and on into the city.

The air was still frosty, and the morning remained grey, but the flat reddish brown fields, laid out in neat rows, were saturated with subtle colour. I passed through small towns and villages, where farmers busied themselves pulling horses and driving heavily burdened tractors. Everyone seemed to be tending to agriculture.

The roads were lined with poplars. Driving a British-made car on the right side along narrow French roads was maddening. It was nearly impossible to see well enough to pass, and I would be stuck for miles behind crawling farm equipment. My lifelong habit of driving on the left frequently caused me to drift into the left lane, from which I had to swerve in sudden frenzy to avoid oncoming traffic.

French driving is often afflicted with madness. Citröens and Deux Chevaux passed at insane speeds. Most French drivers feel that brakes are to be used once a day — for stopping at the end of the journey.

I took a breather in a small village and with a series of grunts and gestures bought bread, cheese, and a small bottle of wine. I ate lunch on the banks of a delightful stream. No food in this world surpasses fresh French bread eaten outdoors beside a tinkling brook.

I wasn't making particularly good time, but I relaxed in the awareness that I had no clock to punch, no schedule, no timetable. I stopped three of four times that afternoon and took in the countryside, just to prove that I had the luxury to do so if I wished.

I picked up the N-1 at Amiens and started making better progress. Just outside Beauvais, I pulled off the main road and had my first dinner at a "Routiere" French café. After a delicious three course meal accompanied by wine, cheese, and fruit, I sat in the corner of the noisy restaurant sipping coffee and sketching the diners. Most were truck drivers or local farmers taking their evening meal after a day's work.

My virgin sketch book began filling up nicely. The room was noisy and animated, and I listened with an air of satiated detachment to jokes and exchanges in the language that I knew I would have to learn sooner or later. The task seemed insurmountable. I am convinced that French and English mouths are constructed differently. The French twirl words with the tongue, while the British speak more from the throat. The most striking difference is in the delivery. The British mumble their words, embarrassed to be heard speaking with passion about a subject. The French present their sentences with drama. A simple phrase is aired with much the same vigor as Olivier delivering Shakespeare.

French cafés are like small vignettes from an ongoing play. They all have roughly the same cast. You will find the Patron, probably the owner, positioned at a strategic corner of the bar, from where he can view the entire production and make adjustments as necessary. The Bar Lady is normally on the plump side, jolly, efficient, and a crack shot with razor-sharp retorts. The control center of the operation, her function is to keep drinks flowing, pure and simple. Nothing is more important to the Patron because such is the basis of a profitable establishment. The Bar Lady has a photographic memory for names, and for the drinks that accompany them.

Waiters are usually male, dressed impeccably in white coat, bow tie, and black trousers. My table was one of twenty or so, and there were only two waiters handling the room. No customer felt a lack of attention.

An accomplished waiter moves with style and flourish. Balancing platters of soup up and down both arms whilst carrying wine bottles and condiments with the hands must be simultaneously carried out with no apparent effort. This requires acrobatic upper body agility and deft footwork.

Waiters must also be master psychologists. They are responsible for making sure that each table orders, eats, drinks, and finishes as quickly as possible-while making sure that customers feel relaxed enough to leave a healthy tip. A good waiter can make the evening. A bad waiter can spoil it.

All cafés have a resident cast of customers, who arrive punctually day after day. They have their regular drinks and customary meals, and unless France wins a major sporting event or experiences an unseasonable turn of climate, their conversation is more or less unchanged from month to month. Without the regulars, the stage would be empty, so they receive discreet, preferential treatment. The Patron, directing from slightly off stage center, makes sure that a glass of their favorite "tonic" is from time to time on the house. Regular customers know almost as much about the workings of the café as the Patron, and have a proprietary interest in making sure that nothing disrupts the routine. Strangers such as myself are tolerated. After all, the café is open to the public and there will always be passers-by. But it takes months or even years before one can become accepted as a regular.

The cozy café, the wine, and my day's travel began to make my eyes bleary. Warm and comfortable, I was sorely tempted to take a room upstairs for the night, but such extravagance would have to be resisted. My budget would not tolerate it.

I paid the bill, climbed back into my van, and searched out a good spot to park for the night. I found a layby at the side of the road just outside town and parked well out of sight, adjusting the load in the rear of my van and unrolling my sleeping bag.

A few hours later I was awakened from a deep sleep. Where was I? What time was it? As I eased myself to full consciousness, I thought I felt the van move. Yes! There it was again! A definite jostle.

I heard a loud thump on the back window and with my heart pounding scrambled into the driver's seat. An enormous face peered at me through the misted windscreen.

I kept a large machete under the driver's seat, a holdover from my military days in the Far East. I had to act. Gripping the oversized knife, I slowly lowered the driver's window.

The face was gone. In its place was a ragged, furry shape with a repulsive odour. I heard a hiss and a moment later encountered an even more nauseating smell. A torrent of foul dark liquid sprayed the window, and a long tail lashed my face. I let out a stifled shout, half scream, half laugh. I was in the middle of a herd of cows.

As I stepped from the van and eased the cows out of harm's

way, I saw in the growing morning light that my vehicle was covered in bits of grass and liquefied cow dung.

The farmer tending the cows looked at me, then the van, then back at me. "*Bonjour*," he said with a thin smile as he moved the slow caravan down the road.

"*Bonjour* yourself," I muttered under my breath.

I spent the next hour cleaning off remnants of the passing herd.

4

Road to the Cote d'Azur

I arrived in Paris at midday. At the outskirts of the city, along the maze of street and freeway intersections, everyone else seemed to know exactly where they were going. I certainly didn't. Lunatic drivers honked and shouted, all but driving me off the road. I had to make one quick decision after another, and it was exhausting work trying to decipher the clutter of highway and street signs. I placed an open map of the city on the passenger seat, but reading it and driving at the same time were next to impossible.

All at once I found myself in the Place de Concord — way, way off course. I had no choice but to drive around, hoping to recognize a street name that would put me in the general direction of Menilmontant.

Suddenly I heard a thumping sound coming from the forward regions of the van. Had I hit something? Had something hit me?

My van abruptly lurched sideway across traffic. Cars screeched and braked. I watched a dizzying panorama of vehicles veer across my windscreen.

Coming to rest halfway across a footpath running parallel to the street, inches from a metal guard rail, I wiped the sweat from my face and opened the door. As I exited, two gendarmes examined me. The orange van, still showing evidence of my battle with the cows, sat breathing heavily, its front nearside tire humiliatingly flat.

The gendarmes began babbling at me and making all sorts of gestures. I tried a little of my halting French. *"Je parle pas French at all je sweez anolais."* This was followed by my finest smile. If anything, this seemed to infuriate them. *"Papier, Monsieur!"* I showed them my license, insurance, international green card, etc., etc. They were having a right old time at my expense. Is it illegal, after all, to have a flat tire? They finally returned the papers and with a final torrent of unintelligible French, sauntered away.

Within hours, my traumatic arrival in the city was forgotten. I spent a delightful week in Paris rummaging through the shops and drinking domestic beverages in the cafés. I gazed upward from the steps of Sacré Couer, basked in the magnificence of the Louvre, drank in the radiance of this uniquely beauteous city.

How appropriate that I should visit Paris immediately upon my recommitment to painting. What other city could have cradled and suckled the arts as she has through the centuries? What other single city could have produced a Pissarro, a Rodin, a Monet, a Picasso?

The atmosphere breathed fire and life. I strolled the streets the immortals had walked. When I closed my eyes, I could hear hansom cabs and see Toulouse-Lautrec Moulin Rouge dancers, Utrillo houses, Degas ballerinas.

The cafés, the cobblestone streets, the shops, the swagger of the city — it was a tonic. Just breathing the air filled me with joy. But I felt that I had to move on, head south, find a place to set up a studio, and embark on my painting.

As the spring mist lifted from the city one raw March morning, I made my way to the N-7 and headed south. The first day out from Paris was uneventful. The road was crowded and my progress again slow (this before the advent of L'Autoroute). I was obliged to drive with caution, sitting in a righthanded vehicle in a lefthanded country. I found myself lagging, breathing diesel fumes as I followed helplessly behind oversize trucks and lorries.

I decided to try a less traveled route and at Moulins left the N-7. I took the road for Clermont-Ferrand, which I reached late in the afternoon. It was already getting dark and the air smelled like approaching rain, but I decided to push on.

My map gave no contour indications, and I was not aware that I was starting to climb the Massive Central. After a couple of hours, the road grew steeper. I was down to second gear most of the time, and the rain was peppered with snow.

I stopped for a quick dinner in a little town not even on the map. It was getting late and I had a decision to make. Should I press on and hope that the route would become more navigable, or stop and find a room for the night?

In my youthful naivete, I decided to drive through the night, maybe catching a catnap in the van. Visions of the palm trees and summer flowers of the Côte d'Azur danced in my head like the snow flakes still fluttering around the van as I climbed back into the driver's seat.

By two o'clock in the morning, I regretted my decision. Snow was falling heavily, and I had been climbing steeply on angry roads for the last three hours. The air was frigid. My heater was gasping for a break. It seemed that I was on top of a mountain — and nothing is darker or more forsaken than a mountain at night in a snowstorm.

The mind plays tricks when driving alone in the early hours before dawn. My vision seemed crystal clear, much more so than usual. Yet the snowy trees and dark, angular shadows had an unworldly aura about them, as if I had been cast into a hellish stage play in which I was the only actor. Taking another sip of brandy, I imagined myself in a warm bed, comfortable in the surety that breakfast with toast and tea would be waiting upon a leisurely awakening.

I shook my head. I had to keep alert. This was clearly not the best of situations. On I drove, the fresh snow so deep that the underside of my crankcase scraped the top, making driving sluggish and strenuous.

In my fatigue, I began to become hypnotized by the windscreen wipers. They swished back and forth with numbing regularity. Large flakes of snow caught on the glass, then were swept away by each ensuing stroke. I drifted into memory, thinking of other roads, other snows.

In early March of my twelfth year, Stavely was covered with

thick drifts. No one could recall such a long, hard winter. My father, who had contracted rheumatic fever as a child, had been smitten with pleurisy and a valvular disease of the heart shortly after I was born. As the snows deepened, his hold on life was ending. Mother knew, and although she didn't speak with me about it, I understood.

One morning the end seemed especially near. Mother asked me to run to the vicarage and tell the priest my father had asked for holy communion. I put a large balacalva on my head, Wellington boots and fat stockings on my feet. Plowing through the blizzard and waist-high drifts, I finally arrived at the vicarage.

"Please, sir. Mum says can you come and give communion to me dad? E's in bed."

In response, the vicar waved his arms and went into a tirade about how sinful it was not to attend church regularly. "If your father wants communion," he shouted, walking away with finality, "he should come and get it!"

I trudged home with a burning knot in my stomach, no longer feeling the cold. Mother was understandably furious, cursing the vicar and his church — house and all.

My father survived that day, and the next. The snow began to thaw. My mother and I remained in the house, awaiting the inevitable. We heard an unexpected knock at the door. Mother opened it and stared openmouthed as the vicar casually asked for items that could be sold in the church jumble sale — old clothing, unused cans of food, jam jars, anything of value. He left with an earful and was lucky not to have collected a black eye.

A week later, in the early hours of a freezing March morning, I was awakened by hysterical weeping. Afraid to move, knowing what had happened, I listened to the hushed scurrying of neighbors in and out of the house.

For some reason, my tears would not come. Perhaps the years of watching my father's health decline had anesthetized me. I felt alone, insecure, incomplete.

Several days later, neighbours and friends made their way to the church in a slow procession. After the ceremony, the vicar, the very same jam-jar-collecting vicar, strolled over to me. He patted me on the head and said, "Well done, my lad!" What he meant I have no idea. My anger, fear, and frustration got the better of me. I kicked out hard with my right foot, catching him squarely on the shin. (My dad the soccer player would have been proud!) The vicar slipped backward and half fell into the open grave. Serves him right, I thought. . .

. . . and finally the tears came.

Driving through the storm in pre-dawn darkness, I shook my head, trying to stay awake.

I was certain that I had taken a wrong turn somewhere along. I hadn't seen a marker for several hours. There were no signs of civilization, and if there had been I might not have seen them because nearly a foot of snow had accumulated.

Options crept through my mind. Stopping and sleeping in the van, I might freeze to death. The temperature was certainly in the single digits Fahrenheit. I had no choice but to keep going. Thank God the van was running well and I had half a tank of gas and half a bottle of brandy.

Driving carefully, I passed some sort of radar tower. Then, without warning, the road swerved sharply left, then right, then left again.

The van veered and was half-pitched into a ditch. I panicked, certain that I would become stuck in the deep powder, but the front-wheel drive took hold and I plowed forward, steering back onto the road.

I continued onward for a moment, greatly relieved, then realized that I was headed downhill. I must have passed over the crest of the mountain, marked perhaps by the radar tower. Now, instead of climbing steeply, I was going downhill and gathering speed.

I eased my foot on the brake.

Nothing happened.

I hit it again, harder this time, pressing it to the floor.

Nothing. The road was like an ice rink. My brakes had no grip at all. I slid onward, gathering speed, careening from snowdrift to snowdrift at either side of the road. I clutched the wheel with white knuckles, but I was no longer in control. My van screamed downhill like a bobsled.

I realised how people must feel before being executed. On I skidded, for long minutes, until I was moving sixty miles per hour or more. I was afraid that I would sail completely over one of the drifts and land in deep snow hopelessly buried, or hit a tree straight on and be done for.

Finally, ice gave way to snow and my brakes caught. I pulled to a stop, covered in sweat. My breath had entirely steamed up the windows. The van itself seemed to be panting. I finished off the brandy, not trusting myself to drive.

After ten or fifteen minutes, I continued on. Again, what choice had I? The road continued to descend, but the snowfall stopped, and I could see the light of dawn. I pulled off at the first village, put my head back, and fell asleep without moving from the driver's seat.

Hours later I awoke from a crippling sleep. My bones and muscles ached as though they had been in combat. My attempt at the world's downhill ski record, combined with the consumption of most of the brandy, had left me with a pounding headache. How could I have been so stupid, I wondered, to drive over a mountain at night in a snowstorm?

On reflection, I realized that I was lucky to have come through alive. This rationale made me feel a little better. So what if I had a hangover? I turned the key and was pleased to hear the van still purring. No lasting damage, at any rate. I filled the tank at the first gas station and had coffee and a croissant. Consulting my map, I found that I was close to Arles. The nightmare route I had taken in the night seemed innocent enough on paper, but I vowed not to get caught in such doltishness again.

I was still travelling downhill, but snow and rain were far behind. The countryside was beginning to become cultivated and summer-like. I dipped down a very steep hill and abruptly found myself in a little village right out of a Van Gogh.

Palm trees swayed and sparkled in the morning sunlight. Vineyards in the distance stretched languidly to the vanishing point. White and pink houses with viridian shutters seemed always to have been there, asking why anyone would choose to live anywhere else. Suntanned residents, dressed in shorts, strolled casually through the streets, shopping in the market and chatting or taking coffee in the outdoor cafés.

I had never seen so much *joie de vivre* in one place. I parked the car and got out to take a closer look. It was about eleven o'clock and already very warm. I strolled along, getting into the casual flow of it all. The sky was bluer than any blue could be. The colours were intense, clear and clean, straight from the tube. The language was music. The pungent perfumes of herbs and flowers were all pervading.

I came to rest at a café near the edge of the square. I had coffee and paté and fresh bread, which hadn't traveled far. The bakery next door filled the air with a sweet smell.

This was the Côte d'Azur.

Palm trees above me filtered the sunshine, hanging like umbrellas. Oregano, red wine, old Deux Chevaux's, *boulangeres, patissaries, charcuteres,* tiny churches with cool interiors, houses like paintings, everywhere Cezanne, Van Gogh, Signac, Ravel, Bizet, and me — sitting in a daze.

The bread was like a religious experience.

5

Ramatuelle

It seemed as though I had been travelling for months, although it had been less than two weeks since leaving the blizzard conditions of London.

In contrast, the Côte d'Azur was a magical garden. It basked contentedly in richness and beauty, embraced with a blanket of warmth and jollity. Still early spring, a feeling of festive summer filled the air. Vanished were grey days, grey suits, and grey spirits. Gone were drab winter clothing and cityscapes with isolated figures scurrying through the cold.

People on the Côte d'Azur moved more slowly. I sensed no urgency, as though contentment was to be savored here and now. This was definitely a Mediterranean locale. Clothes were hung from windows to dry. Daily chores were completed leisurely, with time to chat, think, appreciate.

I drove on along the Mediterranean coastline toward Ramatuelle, a village that a friend in London had assured me I must not miss. Ramatuelle is in the low hills about twelve kilometers inland from St. Tropez. I had no idea what I would find there, but it was at least a destination. If it suited my fancy, I intended to search out a place there to live and paint — that's all I had in the way of a master plan.

I wove along the twisting road following the coast. From

time to time the azure, sparkling water peeked through the trees, leading me onward. I passed through tiny resort towns with enchanting names: Le Lavendue, Cavalaire, and Croix Valmer, until in midafternoon my destination was reached.

My first glimpse of the village, framed by scrub pine, took me by surprise. I rounded a gentle curve in the road, and there sat Ramatuelle high on a hill, twinkling in the afternoon sun, smiling down on the plain which spread out below like a patchwork quilt to the distant sea. The church bell, muffled by the distance, rang the hour at three. A shimmering haze hung over the houses, and wisps of smoke rose lazily from a few of the chimneys.

The village is a classic example of Saracen fortress architecture. A thousand years ago it was built — as were many towns and villages of the region — as a castle, a fortress against marauding hordes. To date, it has withstood even the ultimate horde, that most tenacious enemy: the contemporary international tourist.

Ramatuelle nestles on the side of a rocky hill studded with pine and olive trees, shimmering like a precious faceted stone on the crusty finger of an old dowager. The thick walls and ramparts have had centuries to ripen, wearing their patina like a glow from within. The faded orange tile roofs, impasto walls, and bleached shutters tumble higgledy-piggledy in a haphazard cascade down the hillside, clustering close for company, dancing a slow minuet in the blistering Mediterranean sunshine.

Ramatuelle falls into the category of *village perche,* a perched village. And perched it is. At first glance, it seems as though the village will slide down the hill, so precarious is its nest. But it has no intentions of such a slide. Those buildings have been there a long, long time. They have watched and waited. The village is a survivor. Ramatuelle has seen a few things.

I got out and stood by my little van to take in the full effect. Over the years since, I have made many attempts in my paintings to capture that view, but never again have I been able to possess the feeling of that special day. That moment is alive only in my heart's memory; I don't know if I will ever be able to express it sufficiently.

It's probably just as well.

I stood for an hour transfixed, mesmerized by the changing light on the ancient buildings. I felt that I had come home, that I was returning to something I had known long ago. There was a sudden chill in the air. The sun had fallen behind the hill. I made the final descent to the village and parked in the cozy square. I had no idea what lay ahead, but I was ready for the challenge.

When one puts oneself out on a limb, takes a chance, rolls the dice, it seems that fate either ignores you — in which case you take a fall — or else it reaches out and says, "Okay, this time you deserve a helping hand."

I arrived in the village speaking almost no French. I had about twenty-five pounds remaining. My worldly goods were in the back of my van — a guitar, an easel, a roll of canvas, a box of oil paints, a sleeping bag, a small mattress, a bag of shirts, and a couple pairs of jeans. I considered myself as far out on a limb as I could get. But within a month, I had found a wine cellar in which to live and paint. And I had located a London friend, Peter, who temporarily gave me paying work helping him with a house conversion.

The days were warm and sunny, evenings full of the fragrance of pine smoke. I had no definite plans, but everything was filled with a sense of peace.

I set to fixing up the wine cellar, which had an entrance at street level. Twenty-nine Rue de Centre had a nice ring to it. As the name suggests, the street was the central thoroughfare of the village, leading from the arched entrance, past the post office and the *boulangerie,* and round the corner to the antique shop. The street was about eight feet wide, laid with small boulders from the hills. Over the centuries, these stones had been burnished smooth by the tread of innumerable passers-by.

Rue de Centre was cool even in the heat of summer. It was shaded by three-story buildings with stucco walls, high windows, and terraces hung with pots of flowers. Opposite my little studio, an elderly lady, retired from teaching school, cultivated a garden of morning glories encircling her entire house.

With Peter's help, I installed a shower and toilet and an improvised kitchen. The walls of the cellar were solid stone about six feet thick. My rooms were cool in the day and warm at night. Thick beams ran across the ceiling, the wood so seasoned that nails merely bent when I tried to hammer them in. The cellar was probably about six hundred years old. It was solid, like a part of the earth. I was in touch with the roots of Ramatuelle.

My "studio" was ready.

6

The Port Police

I went right at my work, painting day and night. With the stultifying intensity of London behind me, I felt myself gaining creative strength. For long stretches of every day I was able to pour all my energy onto the canvas. I began to feel alive again, getting back to something I had turned away from years before. I was grateful that it had not passed me by entirely.

My studio was soon well stocked. I produced twenty or so pieces on a variety of surfaces, ranging from proper stretched canvas to discarded grocery boxes.

Although my paintings improved with every new start, making a living selling my work was proving difficult. Every afternoon I would await the arrival of strolling tourists, but it was still early season, and only a few visitors straggled into my studio. Mostly they smiled, nodded, mumbled compliments, and went on their tourist way. I began thinking of my studio as a museum, rather than a gallery, with my role merely to preserve, dust, and watch over the Hallam Collection.

Materials were expensive, and most of my brushes were down to their last hairs. The larder was beginning to suffer, too. I found myself eating reworked soups and an increasing amount of pasta. My supply of vitamin pills was rattling in the bottom of the jar.

The moment of truth arrived as I shook the last two centimes out of my tin. I had been careless. I should have dealt with the problem sooner. Peter had given me a few day's work helping with a building project in the village, but he had returned to London to restock his funds.

I was left to my own devices.

The only solution I could think of was to drive to St. Tropez and set up my display on the waterfront, hoping to attract well-heeled passersby. I had no papers to work in France so this would be risky, but one must follow when the devil drives.

Piling my paintings into the little orange minivan and strapping my easel to the top, I set off for St. Tropez with empty pockets and considerable apprehension.

The Port, an upscale area of shops and restaurants adjoining St. Tropez proper, was just awakening when I arrived. The delicious aroma of fresh coffee and hot croissants made it hard to concentrate on unloading. I set up my easel and paints with a spastic coordination that would have done credit to *Le Comedie Francaise,* and went to work trying to put hunger and thirst out of my mind. Setting up a fresh canvas looking out over the water at the fabulous yachts anchored to the pier, I made a nice start with my oils. Getting excited, I kept my mind on it (and off my hunger) and the painting progressed well.

It was too early in the day for any action from passing tourists. A dog came by and lifted its leg on one of my canvasses, much to the delight of the old men taking the morning sun on a facing bench. I tried to join in their humour as I hosed down the painting. No harm done, but it was somehow ominous in view of my condition.

The morning sun was bright and strong, the sky solid blue cobalt with a hint of turquoise. The noise of the little harbour picked up as the daily bustle of life began to click into gear.

Fishing boats bobbed on the still water. A boat was making its way to the harbour entrance, trailing the faint smell of diesel as it put out for the day's task. Shops opened and cafés started to fill. The natives read the *La Provencal* in the cool shade of bars. The air sweetened with *pastis* and *mais* cigarettes. Seagulls circled the town and chattered and squeaked by the fishing boats. The morning sauntered along, my sale of paintings not keeping pace.

By twelve noon it was uncomfortably hot. I had talked with

a couple of strolling tourists, but had not made a sale. I was feeling weary, depressed, and very hungry. This was not good at all.

I finished off my water bottle and had it grudgingly refilled in one of the cafés. The young woman behind the bar seemed to see right through me — artist, no money, hungry, few prospects.

Returning to my spot, I found two other artists setting up a little way down from me. They were evidently less desperate than I because they had waited until a civilized hour to begin hawking their wares. I walked over to their displays, looked at their paintings, and made a rather awkward effort at introduction. They were French and in no mood for social niceties. This was business.

I returned to my spot, foreign and humble. Getting hungrier by the minute, I continued working on my painting. The crowd was beginning to fill out, and I felt that there may be cause for optimism yet.

By two o'clock I was as penniless as when I climbed out of bed. It was some consolation that the other artists were not making sales either, but by now there were half a dozen of us at intervals along The Port.

My pale London skin began to fry. My nose was the colour of cooked lobster, my lips dry and chapped. I made a hat from a newspaper and finished the painting — not at all bad. I placed it on the easel foremost among my others, thinking that it might offer the best chance for sale since a potential buyer could look right out at the view represented in the painting. I was so thirsty by that time that I couldn't drink enough water to keep even. I flopped into the shade of my minivan and was about to fall into a fitful doze when I felt something pulling at my foot.

"*Monsieur?*"

A young woman was tugging at my shoe.

"*Monsieur, vous etes l'artist?*"

I sat upright, my head smacking hard into the roof of the van.

"*Oui,*" I mumbled.

"*Le piece sur le chevalier?*" She indicated my still-wet painting on the easel.

Her smile was utterly engaging. She was cool and lovely, dressed impeccably, her long blonde hair as carefree as the St. Tropez weather.

"*Ces tres bien. Quesque ces le medium?*" she asked, inquiring about the medium I had used.

I fumbled with my pitiful French.

"*Vous n'est pas Francais?*" she asked.

"*Non. Suis Anglais,*" I replied.

"Oh. Well, I am from Belgium. We can speak English, if you like."

"That would be better," I agreed.

"How much are you asking for the painting?"

My heart pounded — she was perhaps serious.

"I'm sure it's worth several hundred francs," I said. "But I would take eighty for it." In those days that was about ten dollars. My tongue was dry and I felt weak.

"I'll give you fifty," she countered, beaming.

Oh God. Not enough for food, water, coffee, shade. My heart sank.

"Perhaps we could split the difference? How about seventy?"

She giggled and politely writhed inside her dress, moving a little closer and breathing perfume and female all over me.

"Sixty," she practically whispered in my ear.

I casually held onto the van roof for support.

"Sixty-five." My voice was two tones higher than when I had begun.

"Done!"

I took a breath, composing myself.

"It's still very wet," I said.

"Yes?" She reached out with a well-manicured finger and dabbed at a corner of the painting. Her fingertip came back light blue.

"So it is," she smiled, holding her blue finger erect.

I reached into my painting box and pulled out an old rag.

"Allow me." I wiped off the blue with a little turpentine, polishing and buffing the end of the exquisite digit.

"Could you perhaps deliver?" She demurely retrieved her finger.

I asked if she were staying in town.

"A little way out on the beach road." She drew a small map on my sketch pad.

"All right. The day after tomorrow, say around five in the afternoon?" I offered.

"That's fine. I'll be back from the beach." She turned to leave.

"Could you perhaps leave a deposit?" I asked as casually as I could, swallowing hard.

"Oh! Silly of me. I forgot."

She reached into her bag and pulled out a fat roll of bills. She peeled off the entire sixty-five francs and handed them to me.

"*A bien tot!*" She flashed her dazzling smile and sauntered away, leaving my moist hands clutching the lovely money.

It took all my willpower, but I waited until she had floated out of sight before diving into the café and inhaling several coffees and a large omelette.

I settled back into the café chair. For the first time in a week I felt at peace with the world. I had eaten well, had sold a painting, and had a little money in my pocket. With any luck, I was well on the way to a rendezvous with a gorgeous lady.

Life was as sweet as my coffee.

When I returned to my easel, two gendarmes were waiting. They smiled thin, professional smiles and touched their hats in a perfunctory salute.

I was English, yes? The passport please. The van — mine? The papers. The green card. You are staying in an hotel? Oh — in a house. Your own? You rent?

You sell paintings? How much? Ah so.

You will please come with us.

I was alarmed. What had I done? I protested, but with my halting French I was lost.

I packed my paintings and easel into the van and locked it. All eyes followed as I was escorted to police headquarters at the far end of The Port.

A dour little man with neat sideburns, a large mustache and pig-like, humourless eyes took down the particulars. I was instructed to empty my pockets. They scooped everything into a tray, and I was briefly frisked, no doubt to make sure that I had no brushes or tubes of alizarin crimson concealed in or about my British personage.

I was becoming decidedly uncomfortable and angry, but scared, as any self-respecting artist would be. The coffee and omelette were making their way toward the nearest exit.

In a quaking voice I protested my treatment, demanding to see the British Consulate (the nearest was probably in Paris). This had no effect whatsoever, and I found myself pushed into a jail cell.

I—in jail!

The cell was about ten feet square, smelling of old wine and stale urine. Flies buzzed continually. Probably even they were afraid to land in such filth. A single naked bulb hung from the ceiling. Two bunks were placed head to foot along adjoining walls. One had an occupant who was in quiet conversation with a chair. I could make out the French words for police and idiots and fuck off. He had a three-day growth of stubble on his chin and rags for clothing. Apparently he was not aware of my entrance, for which I was grateful.

It was chilly in the dank cell, and I began to panic. The sale of my painting certainly was at the bottom of this, but to be tossed in the pokey seemed a bit extreme. I had heard hair-raising tales about police brutality in foreign countries, about barbarous beatings and generally despicable behavior by the "flic."

An hour passed. The gendarmes were enjoying a joke at the far end of the hall outside my cell, their group swathed in blue clouds of cigarette smoke that was cast through with shafts of late afternoon sunlight.

I distinctly remember that a fly buzzed round the room and that a large clock on the wall ticked like an enormous monstrous metronome.

"Assume position," the headmaster said.

I had been prepped beforehand on what to do. Without dropping my trousers, I bent down and grabbed my ankles.

Whoosh!

The pain was excruciating. My trousers tore, leaving me naked to the lash.

Civilized societies have deemed caning unacceptable as a

means of discipline and have confined it to the darker corners of the globe. Yet it was used, sparingly, at my grammar school. My arrest for stripping lead from the church roof was a third and final offense. (Roof leading at that time was quite valuable.) At the age of fifteen, I was sentenced to four blows on the buttocks and one on the palm of each hand.

Swoosh! The second blow.

The pain seeped into my groin. This was going to be worse than I had imagined. From nowhere, I had a vision of my father as a young man playing cricket, laughing with his teammates. I could see his face clearly, more vivid even than my memories of his final days. A full head of hair, ruddy cheeks, and a broad smile. I had never seen him that way in life, but I would keep that picture in my head. Dad would get me through.

Whack!

The third blow struck with even greater intensity. Pain crept like clawed fingers up into my stomach and down into my legs. Tears involuntarily started to well.

My father on the cricket field, brave, tall, playing through the pain.

Thwack!

The final blow. My buttocks, groin, and lower stomach were numb beyond pain. I thought of my father. There he was, smiling right in front of me.

I had trouble trying to stand upright. My body didn't seem to work.

The headmaster stared down at me with an almost quizzical expression. I wondered to myself: "Has he ever been caned? Does he understand? How could anyone do this to someone if he had gone through it himself?"

"Well, Hallam, are you all right?" He glowered at my snivelling.

"Please, sir. Yes, sir," I blubbered.

"Right hand!"

I held out my right hand, palm upward.

Whack went the cane and almost immediately a large red welt appeared. The headmaster motioned for the other hand.

Thwack.

A similar red welt came up.

It was over.

I took stock. I was still alive. Able to breathe. I had no sensation in my buttocks and groin.

"Right, Hallam. Now, you know why you've been punished. Contrary to what you might think, we do not enjoy caning our boys. It's a nasty business all round, but stealing from the church cannot be left unpunished. I want to see you buckle down to some real work next term. I shall be watching you closely. All right, you may leave."

It was more than a week until I could sit without discomfort.

After the caning, the task of regaining a grip on my perverse ways was assisted by an onslaught of yellow jaundice. My liver packed up and went on holiday, leaving my digestive system unable to cope with anything more demanding than boiled fish, which I was fed at nearly every meal. To this day I cannot abide boiled fish.

The confinement in bed, however, allowed me to catch up on my school work. By the end of my illness, I was astounded at how rewarding the business of learning could be. It's not that I particularly enjoyed study, but that I found satisfaction from piecing together bits of unconnected information.

It took three terms of diligent work, but by the time final high school examinations came around, the wastrel had done it. At the age of sixteen I was top of my class, and it began to look as if there was hope for us all.

My cellmate had fallen asleep. I sat despairingly on the end of the other bunk. The flies never let up with their incessant buzzing.

Finally, an older man entered the station. The others greeted him with deference. Cigarettes were put out and uniforms adjusted. All at once everyone tried to look busy. He was unmistakably the chief.

He shuffled through the papers on his desk, drumming his fingers. After much pondering and sighing, he signaled to have the wretched English painter brought before him. As they released me from the cell, I told them that I would like a pee and a drink, in that order. I tried to sound as calm as possible, but my voice had an uncomfortable flutter.

The older man spoke halting English but ignored my requests.

"Monsieur, you are ze English and 'ave no aussority to work in ze France. Zis is a zerious affair."

He ran his fingers down his long nose and pulled his mustache.

"I am informed that you were zeen conductin' a tranzaction on ze Port earlier today. Zis is zo?"

He leaned back in his squeaky chair.

"Well — er — I suppose that's true," I said. "But—"

I was cut short.

"You were conductin' ze business 'ere in ze France."

"Well—" I really had nothing to say in my own defense.

"Zis is not allowed. You 'ave broke in French law. Yes? No? Yes."

"I didn't know," I mumbled. My resolve and calmness evaporated. I envisioned myself shipped off to the Foreign Legion or a penal colony in the Caribbean.

A long pause. He examined the money found in my pocket, my sketchbook, my passport, my wallet, my Swiss army knife.

Abruptly he pushed them across the desk. "My advice, monsieur, is to remain in your village, stay off my Port. *Ca va?*"

Before I could say a word, I was bundled out into the street, rather like a stray dog.

It was early evening. The air was sweet and clear, spiced with oregano and barbecue. Aperitifs were being taken in the cafés. Early diners were assembling for the nightly battle with the cornucopia of gourmet food.

I was free.

A close call — but all's well that ends well. I probably would have kissed the chief if I'd had the chance.

I sat with a large cognac and a heart overflowing with gratitude. Close calls seem to produce a reverence for life, which is otherwise taken completely for granted.

7
Insult to Injury

Two days later, I delivered the painting. The blonde patron was just as blonde and just as disturbing as at our meeting on The Port. She greeted the doorbell wearing the most minimal of bikinis. The effect was calculated to be devastating, and was more than successful.

I presented her with the finished painting, by this time dry and varnished. It was one of my better pieces. I hated to see it go, but she had paid for it in good faith, and I had already spent some of the money.

Dragging me inside by the hand, she lavished praise and showed me where the painting would hang. She offered me *pastis*, and we sat by her pool chatting about this and that. She seemed genuinely interested in my work, where I came from, and what I was hoping to do with my painting career.

Gathering courage, I decided to try my luck. I made a clumsy and not very subtle attempt at a dinner invitation. To my astonishment, she said that she would be delighted to meet me that evening.

"I'll see you at L'Escale, say, seven o'clock?" she said, flashing her exquisite smile. I kissed her hand debonairly and staggered out the door, nearly tripping on the step down to her gravel driveway.

I felt intoxicated. This was my first date in French. By quarter to seven I ensconced myself at a strategic table at L'Escale. I had arrived early, taking no chances with my temperamental minivan.

I was beginning to feel uneasy by ten after. No sign of my date. Then all at once she was sitting across from me, looking cool and lovely in a white dress, her brown skin soft and embraceable.

She leaned over the table and kissed me on the cheek. "Where are you taking me then?" she whispered.

I had forgotten that we were there for a reason. When I didn't respond, she asked sweetly, "What about here?"

My heart stopped. Eating at L'Escale was unheard of. One could have a drink here — if the day had been particularly successful. But eating! I could live for a month on what a salad would cost.

Before I could come up with a plausible reason for seeking out a reasonable bistro round the back of town, she had caught the attention of the maître d' and we were being seated in the restaurant proper.

I had a small salad and drank water. Thinking about the bill with every bite, I doubt if a single shred digested. She had a steak that looked absolutely mouth watering, cheese, dessert, coffee, and cognac.

The bill came to just two francs less than what she had paid me for the painting. Taking into account the meal I had eaten immediately after the sale, I was back to square one, which meant flat broke.

At any rate, the rest of the evening would be wonderful. I had the certain feeling that we would end up back at her villa, dancing on the patio in the warm breeze off the bay, while moonlight shimmered across the pool. We would savor the moment. It would be ours to explore.

After dinner we were sauntering along on The Port when a large white Mercedes pulled alongside us.

"*Cheri!*" she shrieked. "*Oh Cheri! Que'lle surprise. Mais —*" and she leaped into the car, showering the driver with kisses while continuing to babble in French.

"Oh, Kerry, I'm sorry. This is Claude, my husband. He wasn't supposed to be arriving till tomorrow." She turned and planted another wild one on the fortunate Claude.

"Isn't it super that you came early?" she gushed all over him. "Let's get back to the villa right now. I want to show the present I bought you. Ciao, Kerry, thanks for dinner!"

The white car pulled away. Undoubtedly, the present she referred to was my painting.

Why did I not feel honored?

8

Establishing the Studio

The chief of police's admonition, "Remain in your own village," epitomized one of the guardian principles of the police system: if at all possible let someone else deal with the problem. In the immediate vicinity, this meant keeping undesirables out of St. Tropez, and in the surrounding villages.

Over the next few weeks, however, it became clear that by following his advice I could chart a most profitable course of action.

Driving back and forth to a nearby dump, I added a few additional decorative touches to my wine cellar/apartment/ studio/gallery. I laid a concrete floor, installed a front door that actually opened and closed, made shelves, and threw down a rug. My trips to the dump garnered pots and pans, chairs, cupboards, carpets, and so forth. A nail here and a dash of paint there usually made them good as new. As the days progressed, my studio became almost palatial.

I felt that I was on the verge of achieving what I had set out to do — that is, bail out of a drab London life and set myself up in a romantic fairyland of possibilities. All that I had left was to figure out how to support myself.

I knew that I should start to build up a substantial supply of paintings that I could sell once the Season arrived. But I suddenly felt that my paintings weren't good. My palette was full of London mud. My colours kept my style stilted and halting. I was still at Art School!

I had brought with me from London the remnants of a brief flirtation with the American School of Abstract Expressionism. My interest had been spurred by exposure to the New York painters of the late fifties, who seemed to be blazing a tantalizing new artistic trail.

My interest in this trail was more trendy than heartfelt. As with any brief affair, I had gained little of lasting worth. I had never really studied and embraced their philosophy. Now, alone on the Côte d'Azur, with sales meaning survival, my direction was unclear and ill-defined. Swirling clouds of reds and blues mixed in a collage of yesterday's newspaper and smashed tin cans are all well and good if part of a larger continuing exploration. I had to admit that my daubings were pathetic imitations. They lacked conviction and therefore contained little of substance. They had nothing about them that would make the teeth itch.

I thought back to my university years in London. As students, we were thrown all sorts of ideas on technique and style. Most of it was random vagary, but I suppose there was some method to the madness. Professors encouraged us to troop off to as many museums and galleries as we could fit into our hectic curriculum. I now understand that they prayed such an atmosphere would magically hit us over the head, as with a two by four, and we suddenly would see the light of great art.

But sketching hour after hour from the Great Masters becomes tedious. The all-encompassing question always was with us: "Where will this lead?" Reality struck my classmates one by one. I could see it in them, and I myself heard the call all too clearly. "Get a worthwhile occupation before it's too late. Grow up. Forget this childish drivel. Get a job. Get a haircut."

Of the fourteen students who graduated with me, I believe I alone have made any kind of a living from painting. Everyone else drifted into fields less hazardous to the bank account.

Walking from my winecellar to the hills near Ramatuelle one brilliantly clear afternoon, I came to a decision. My old professor would be proud of me. I would return to realistic painting. I would re-examine what Art was all about and find out where I fit in — if at all.

Had not my rendering of the St. Tropez harbour sold immediately? Would not buyers want to purchase paintings that celebrated the natural beauty of this region of the world? The Côte d'Azur. One of the cradles of French Impressionism. The overwhelming luminosity and enchantment of the atmosphere had stimulated artists to produce works that turned the art world on its ear. Everywhere I looked, I saw a painting. I was living inside a masterpiece. I determined that capturing the intrinsic beauty of the Côte d'Azur would become my quest. I would make definitive statements about this landscape, using Van Gogh, Cezanne, Matisse, and Dufy as departure points. I would try to amplify what they saw, build on their feelings, dance to their music.

But in what medium to set it all down? I was using oil paints, which take quite a while to dry, so my output was limited. Before leaving London, I had bought a set of what was then a newfangled-type of paint, called acrylics. There were six tubes in the set — the primaries, white, black, and a burnt sienna.

What the hell, I thought. I'll give them a try. To my surprise and delight, I found the new medium quite to my liking. The paints were flexible, they covered well, and they dried rapidly, meaning that I could place another layer almost immediately. With oils, you sometimes have to wait days for a layer to dry.

I quickly produced a very pleasant series of small paintings on wood panels. I worked outside, right from nature, not minding the sun and wind. I studied the landscape deeply. The hills round my village, the streets and cafes, the village market — all became my domain. I even ventured now and again into St. Tropez, directly painting the shimmering harbour and vibrant street scenes. As long as I didn't try to sell anything, no one would bother me, I correctly assumed.

Gradually, I worked up courage and experience and began setting up my easel on the hills overlooking the Mediterranean, trying to capture the sweeping grandness of mountain and sea. A month passed. Then another. I painted each day until my eyes ached, then tossed myself into bed and fell instantly asleep, only to dream of painting as though I were still standing before a canvas. I seemed to learn even while asleep. Hardly ever have I gone through such a period of sustained artistic growth.

9

First Season on the Cote d'Azur

T he tourist season moved into full swing, and word
seemed to get out that an interesting British artist lived,
and had a gallery, in a reconverted wine cellar.

In a moment of inspiration, I invested in a gallon of the local rosé and positioned it in a decorative ice boat near the door. I placed a full glass in the hand of every prospective buyer. On a hot day, it was hard to resist a cooling glass of this nectar. Its sweetness encouraged a second glass, and at that point the defenses became anesthetized.

The wine proved a sound investment. Almost twenty proof, it was the catalyst for more than a few sales. Small sketches, watercolours, and the odd acrylic and oil flew out the door, rapidly restocking the tin can. I was once more solvent and able to relax.

My daily routine assumed an easy pattern. Rise at 7:30. Breakfast on hot croissants and café au lait under the shade of the awning and climbing vines in the village square (or "place," as the locals called it). In the evenings between five and seven, I obliged myself to be open for tourists. The rest of the day was quiet, and when I was not painting I had taken to visiting two friends from London, Anita and Maggie, who worked as wait-resses at one of the fine St. Tropez beach clubs. I would lunch,

take a swim, and enjoy some sunshine before returning to re-
ice the rosé for the five o'clock rush.

Life in this small village was ordered and balanced. Not
much had changed in the last five hundred years, and I had
the impression that not much probably would in the next five
hundred. Over time, a deeply settled groove had etched out a
map with which everyone was familiar. Every villager seemed
to unconsciously understand that straying from the accepted
would be of no profit. The result was predictability and
stodginess, but also an innate and deep-seated strength. Everyone knew what was what — and how to keep it that way.

Ramatuelle was many things to many people. For Madame
Le Farge, who visited regularly, it was a refuge from society
columns. For famous cinema stars, politicians, industrialists,
and other public figures, it was and still is a summer retreat
from the public eye. To local inhabitants, who even during the
height of the Season made up the vast majority of citizens
trodding the streets, Ramatuelle was simply home. Mr. Vin
Rouge was born and doubtless will die there. Jean Le Trick, a
simple man who loved his work, collected the town's refuse
and made sure the streets were clean. Angelique sold groceries, and Madame Sabastine had a gift shop that was never open.

I enjoyed watching the village awake. Each day began much
the same. Workmen fortified themselves with *pastis* and *gitanes*.
Tourists scrutinized maps and planned the day's programme.
The early sun poked at the pots of geraniums and nudged the
cigalons (grasshoppers) into chorus. The scent of brewing coffee mingled with that of the pine hills and Jean's diesel sanita-
tion truck. Village cats made a final check under café tables
before retiring for their morning snooze.

Fairly early every morning, the postman, pickled in Pernod,
swung his yellow Citröen van into a parking place and made
for the sanctity of the café. One of the village miracles was that
mail actually arrived on time each day.

By midmorning, a crowd had usually gathered in the
square. The streetsweeper, the baker, the butcher, the local vint-
ner, the schoolteacher, the garage owner, the real estate agent,
the plumber, and an assortment of other local characters gathered in a reverent group beneath a canopy of trees to honor the

traditional local pastime: *petanque.*

Petanque is a game as old as the sandy ground on which it is played, as ancient as the rocks of the surrounding foothills. It is played with smooth round iron spheres the size of overweight tennis balls. A smaller wooden ball, called a jack, is tossed some distance onto the dirt playing surface, and each player has several attempts to roll one of his balls closest to the jack. The game, which is played one-on-one or as teams, consists of infinite nuances, ploys, blocks, and finesses. It is played throughout France wherever there is a piece of spare ground.

Petanque brings the generations together. It is almost unheard of these days in most industrialized countries for young men to take the time to sit with old codgers discussing local and national events. Yet here they could be seen day after day, young and old, sitting together at café tables after a game, arguing about the outcome and toasting the oncoming evening. In this I could sense mutual respect. It was a tradition tightening the fabric of life. In England we have soccer and cricket. In America football, baseball, and basketball. But none are direct and ingrained into daily life as petanque.

For most, petanque is a wonderful excuse for a quick *pastis* and some slow gossip. Among certain groups, however, it is played with intense passion. I have watched spellbound as elderly French gentlemen become transformed into ravenous wolves kept from each others throats only by the realisation that murder in such circumstances would indeed be embarrassing. Tennis has its aficionados, golf its fanatical devotees, and stamp collecting its savant connoisseurs. None are equal in intensity a group of devoted petanque players, thoroughly lubricated, eyes maniacal, each with a long-dead cigarette stuck permanently to the lower lip, wagering sanity upon the simple attempt to roll one little ball close to another. Petanque showed me that sophistication among the villagers was a facade. Scratch the surface and you would find pure peasant: uncivilized, bigoted, with anger waiting to erupt.

I was soon to discover the fragility of the village's hold on this century.

10

The Barber

Since moving to the village, my existence had been barely acknowledged by the locals. It was beyond their comprehension that a sane person would arrive from London and proudly live in a cellar. It smacked of eccentricity, a dangerous commodity likely to unbalance things. Look out for *Le Fou Anglais*. I paid francs for bread, groceries, meat, and drinks, so grudgingly, I was allowed to stay.

I was not exactly shunned, but close to. I struck up a casual acquaintance with a middle-aged woman named Marie Ange, the village gossip who spoke with me primarily because, I think, she needed to remain informed for her audience. And I had a passing aquaintance with a young woman, the wife of the barber's son. She always smiled and wished me *Bonjour. Bon soir. Ca va?* During my first few months, hers was the only ongoing contact that I had with the village population.

Many afternoons I drove my little orange minivan down to Escalet, where I would take a swim and spend an hour on the sunny beach. One day I left Ramatuelle after lunch, and on the way out of the village saw the wife of the barber's son standing with her bicycle at the side of the road. She waved excitedly and seemed very anxious.

When I pulled over, I managed to grasp that her bicycle was broken and she was late for work, which on that particular day consisted of cleaning *le grande maison,* "the big house" at the end of the road. Could I give her a lift? And when I returned to the village, could I drop off her bicycle at Mr. Arnaud's repair shop?

I was delighted to be of help, thinking that a good deed might improve my standing with the villagers. I dropped her at the entrance of the tree-lined drive leading to the house. She thanked me profusely and skipped off to her cleaning chores.

After an hour at the beach, I returned to the village. As I lifted the bike from my van, I became aware that people were paying me an unusual amount of attention. Turning, I saw the barber and two other large men striding toward me, shaking their fists and growling in angry Provencal. I understood few of their words, but apparently I was not at the moment on their list of favorite people.

The barber stepped forward. With his face inches from mine, he spat more abuse. He grabbed the bicycle and hurled it to the ground.

I tried to smile and protest (in English), which of course made matters worse. The tirade from the three continued: My mother ate shit and my father was a child molester, and on and on. My bumper was kicked and my van rocked. Fists and arms flailed threateningly. To that point, I had not been touched, but I figured it was only a matter of time.

As the trio began to retreat, I caught phrases that jolted me. *Tête comme un ballon. A sept heure. Ce soir. Vach, putane,* etc., etc. The nub of it was that I would be visited and done over at seven o'clock that evening.

The old crones in black who sat on the church walls cackled in my direction. I hurried to Marie Ange, who knew everything to do with life in the village, but she was no help. She tut-tutted, waving a finger from side to side in front of my face. She dismissed me with a chortle and an *Eh-voila,* which had a ring of finality that was not in the least comforting.

I staggered back to the cool comfort of my cave, shaken and truly afraid. I was, after all, in a foreign country — and a rather backward part of it to boot.

The only person I could think to talk with was my friend Dimitri in St. Tropez. He was Russian, tall and gruff, with a Viva Zapata mustache and a menacing grin. He could perhaps help with my problem.

On the drive down to St. Tropez, I mulled over possible courses of action. I could pack and leave before the gang of villains arrived. I could face them alone and try to come out of it alive. I could leave for a few days and hope the whole thing blew over.

I recalled Peter warning me that the locals had strange ideas and even stranger ways of dealing with Kafars — usually involving shotguns and clubs.

I arrived at Dimitri's and was quickly reassured. "This is quite serious, you don't worry for nothing, my friend. We come visit with you tonight and nothing will happen."

I left feeling better, but still disturbed. On the road back to the village, I thought of my waitress friends from London. Anika spoke impeccable French, and I persuaded her to come with me to talk to the barber and his family.

The barber's son answered the door. Anika quickly explained the situation and my fear of being worked over for something I probably hadn't even done. He assured us that this was *pas de problem*, and that his father was "from the old ways." He assured us that he would talk with his father and the gang.

I gave Anika a hug and we made off to the café for a celebratory *pastis*. There we found my friendDimitri, who had arrived early. He was sitting with two swarthy youths. The three looked like a gang of thugs, arms folded, their eyes dark and hard. I quickly explained that the problem had been solved with Anika's help.

"Shit!"Dimitri shouted and looked at me with genuine disappointment. It was as though I had taken away something very precious. He said that he had gone to a lot of trouble getting up there at such short notice, as had his compatriots. He assured me that it was indeed frustrating to have spent so much time and preparation for naught.

He leaned closer and inched open the violin case resting on his lap. I caught a glimpse of the hard dark metal of a submachine gun.

Dimitri had certainly come prepared.

I bought them drinks, and Anika and I watched as they

drove away — a sad trio deprived of their fun.

A few weeks later I found out what really had happened. The wife of the barber's son apparently had been having an affair with the owner of the big house. By helping her, I had been an innocent party to the deception. As far as the barber and his cutthroats were concerned, I was as guilty as she.

I was also English, which compounded my sins.

11

Return to London

By September, I had a well-established "practice" in the village. My first season on the Côte d'Azur, after a few initial hiccups, had gone smoothly, and I had managed to save a little money. Most important, I had accomplished what I had set out to achieve. I had become an artist, not rich and famous certainly, but accomplished in the sense that I had sold many paintings of my own creation. A few buyers had even showed up at my door upon referral. That was gratifying, and I had every reason to think that this would continue. My work, I felt, was gaining strength.

By the beginning of November, the last of the tourists had vanished. Peace and quiet returned to the village. Then things became too quiet. Being a sociable sort, I longed for a good natter, in English, of course. My friends Anika and Maggie had been laid off with the slowing of the tourists and had returned to London. This left me alone with the village locals, who spoke only French — when they spoke to me at all.

Confident that I had squeezed the last drops of income from the season, I decided to pack it up and return to London for Christmas. I arranged with my landlady to store my easels and paints and locked the door behind me, confident that I would return again the following summer.

Arriving in London after a two-day drive, I moved in with

two of my closest friends, Collin and Bill, who shared a maisonette at 43 Redcliffe Gardens. We had the entire top floor, six rooms in all, plus bath and kitchen. It was warm and spacious. Each of us had money to chip in for rent. I had my savings from France, Bill was in display and exhibition construction, and Collin was playing piano in Flannigan's Fish Emporium.

I put together a show of my paintings and was invited to exhibit at a popular and overpriced restaurant in Notting Hill Gate. The show enjoyed a modicum of success. I sold four or five pieces, which accomplished little more than paying for the frames and the meals I found myself eating at the restaurant.

As before in London, I soon felt my artistic energy dissipating. My expenses were running high, and it was difficult to force myself to sit at the easel when the likelihood of selling the finished product was slight.

I was facing straight on, again, the conflict between art and eating. Painting is such a delicate activity, so in tune with the fine chords of the heart, that I found it next to impossible to paint when I was consuming myself with worry.

With great fondness, I often thought about my old art instructor. Every so often, his words swirled round in my mind:

I've every hope that you have what it takes to become a real artist. I mean a real one. A person of vision and integrity, capable of creating significant works of substance and importance.

That's what I wanted. That's what I had worked toward over so many years. But reaching the state of supporting myself through my art was ephemeral, a state of being, floating just out of reach.

Like a cruel joke, at times.

I began picking up a little extra money singing in some of the nearby clubs. The money was peanuts, really, but at least I could count on something at week's end. I had hammered away at my guitar since grammar school, and club owners liked me because my voice apparently was just bad enough to drive customers to drink.

It was tough work. I would arrive at the dinner hour, sit on a stool on stage and sing my heart out for four or five hours, strumming my guitar as energetically as I could with as few breaks as I could manage. Club owners never like performers to take breaks. They feel that the sale of refreshments takes a dip when the music stops. Those were exciting days in the London music world. New stars were discovered every month, and no one knew who would be next. To make up for my lack of painting, I began to write a few tunes. The lyrics were heartfelt, but I realized I had a long way to go before dislodging the Beatles from the top spot. The reality was that I played for drinks and tips — and, as I mentioned, my monkey wages.

12
Thomas Edwards and Son

Just round the corner from our maisonette was a general grocery shop, Thomas Edwards and Son. A remarkable establishment in the old style, it was run by Mr. Edwards, his wife, and their cat. As far as I could tell, there was no son.

Collin, Bill, and I picked up most of our groceries and sundries there. Every visit was an experience. When you pushed open the glass door, a bell rang somewhere in the back. The entire place smelled of dust and garlic. It was nearly dark inside day or night. A couple of naked bulbs hung from the ceiling. The cat normally slept through the day on one of the numerous sacks of oats, rice, or root vegetables.

Mr. Edwards's taste in groceries was eclectic. I'm sure he stocked his store by intuition. What he liked, he carried. There was no indication that he catered in any way to general grocery trends or public demand. Great sides of smoked bacon, festooned with flies, hung from the ceiling alongside bunches of onions, garlic, and dried herbs. His shelves were aclutter with boxes of every kind and colour. Great mounds of butter and cheese lay on marble slabs. Kippers were lined up in glass cases. Jars of pickled onions in precarious stacks sat near boxes of shoe polish, cutlery sets, dishcloths, and long rectangles of soap. The musty smell and dim light gave everything the impression of a stage set.

Mr. Edwards and his wife were always busy. Always. It

took an eternity to be served, even when there were no customers in the store other than myself. The couple, in their matching grocery aprons, seemed engaged in a lifetime of moving things from one place to another, and back again. There was no resulting increase in order, just a different arrangement to the clutter.

One morning Collin came into the kitchen of our upper-floor flat with a brand new box of Rice Pop Crackles, or whatever, and poured a bowl. When milk was added, the cereal turned into a rather blue-gray sludge with greenish moss floating on top.

"What do you make of this?" he asked.

Bill and I both agreed that it was not the most appetizing breakfast we had ever seen. I picked up the box of Rice Pop Crackles and gave it a look. On the back, a big notice proclaimed: "Win a free plastic tulip! Fill in the application and enclose six pence for handling. All entries must be received by 31 December 1954."

It was then 1963.

"Bit over the hill," Bill said.

We agreed that Mr. Edwards had excelled himself this time. Collin was a little perturbed, though. "I'm taking it back. The hell with it. I mean, enough is enough." I could hardly blame him. What if he had taken a bite of the stuff before looking?

I said I'd go with him to make sure satisfaction was gained. Walking round the corner, we pushed open the door. The bell rang and Mr. Edwards, dragging a sack of Midlothian pinhead oats, scrutinized us over the top of his spectacles.

"I bought this packet of cereal this morning and it's off," said Collin.

"Off?"

"Yes, off."

"You mean it's spoiled?"

"It turns green and blue when you add milk."

"No, really? Well, I'm blowed," said Mr. Edwards.

"Furthermore, the date on the back is 1954."

A smile lit Mr. Edwards's wizened face. He pointed to the shelf from which the box had been taken and leaned forward as though about to impart a great secret.

"Yes, well, you see . . . they're very slow movers."

13

Priscilla

A close friend was to be married in a small church in Hampstead. I was invited to the ceremony and reception, along with several hundred others.

The chosen day was freezing cold. Everyone arrived in winter gear, and we filed into the church. The ceremony began, the bride marched down the aisle, and everything was moving along quite well, with the customary ponderous sincerity of the parson and dutiful attention of the audience.

Suddenly the doors at the back of the church swung open, and light from outside flooded the dark sanctuary. Priscilla Downs-Rose, a friend of the bride and groom and slight acquaintance of mine, made her grand entrance. Everyone kept one eye on the proceedings and the other on Priscilla as she floated down the aisle wearing an enormous gorgeous hat and a light pink dress which, despite the frosty day, was very, very short. Flashing a smile here and there, she eased into the pew next to me. Leaning over, she asked me in a throaty stage whisper that could be heard throughout the church, "What's the story so far?"

With this, the parson succumbed. He glared over the top of his glasses at Priscilla and me, fixing us with a withering stare. Completely used to such stares from members of the church, I took it in stride, as did Priscilla, who gave me a conspiratorial wink.

The ceremony drew to its inevitable zenith, and after the couple was pronounced well and truly hitched, guests trooped to the bride's flat for the reception. Priscilla latched onto me, and for the next hour or so we sloshed down wine, devoured hors d'oeuvres, and generally chatted and flirted outrageously. We ended up in a small room at the end of the hall, gasping and groping amid the brooms and brushes.

"Darling," she moaned, "I have to leave. I'm going home for the weekend."

Five more minutes of continued grasping and heavy breathing.

"Really, darling," she cooed, trying to compose herself.

A few more minutes.

"Kerry, darling, I say. . . ."

I was on an irreversible course. Several additional minutes went by, then Priscilla managed to untwine one of my arms and adjust her dress. She did this with no great conviction, but it served to break the continuity and cool the ardor a bit.

"All right," I said, suddenly gallant. "I'll take you home."

"You really don't have to. I mean, I can get a train."

"Nonsense," I insisted.

"Well, you darling man! If you insist, who am I to argue? I simply have to accept, don't I?"

We staggered down the stairs, taking leave of our hosts and pouring ourselves into my well-traveled minivan.

"Are you sure you can drive?" Priscilla asked.

"I could drive a tank if I had to!"

To prove my point, I hurled the van into gear. With a wrenching rattle it leaped forward, engine screaming. Priscilla's dress tangled in the gearshift as we accelerated. I fumbled desperately. She simply threw back her head and laughed.

Minutes later, with the van contentedly in fourth gear, I had a free hand to take up where I had left off in the broom closet. We sped down the road, sipping champagne direct from the bottle, which Priscilla had hidden in her hat as we left.

Half an hour later, it occurred to me that we were somewhere in the north suburbs of London. I inquired where her house was located.

"Oh, darling, I'm going home for the weekend. Daddy's and Mummy's place in Suffolk."

"How far is that?"

"Oh, about another hour, I should say."

I pulled in a layby and got out. "I need to stretch my legs," I said. "And mother nature has to be visited."

We were parked by a large wooded area and were both able to attend to our toilet. The effects of the champagne were somewhat diminished, but our other appetites were as strong as ever. Sweeping aside my art supplies, we rolled into the back of the van and flailed about for half hour or so before getting underway again.

Down the road ten miles or twenty, Priscilla decided that it was time for another flail, so again to the back of the van. The lady was insatiable.

By the time we reached her house it was dark. We were both tired and depressingly sober, with the beginnings of early evening hangovers.

We passed through a large iron gate and proceeded up the stately curving lane to the house. Easing into the gravel driveway, I pulled to a halt behind a Rolls and a Bentley. The house was enormous. Priscilla's father apparently had been a commissioner in some far eastern colony until being booted out for taking colonial policy a little too far. As all good aristocrats seem to do in such circumstances, he returned to England undaunted and full of righteous indignation, to spend the rest of his life looking after his country estate.

"I'll drop you off and go back to London," I said. I didn't feel up to a brush with aristocracy.

"Nonsense, darling. You'll stay over and go back tomorrow."

Priscilla took my reluctant hand, and we swept into the library where Mummy and Daddy were serving after-dinner drinks to the Lord and Lady of the neighboring seat. Upon our entrance they all froze like deer in headlights.

Following their gaze, I looked at Priscilla. Her mascara was smeared all over her face. Her lipstick, most of which was probably on my shirt, was smudged across her cheeks and chin like the doodlings of a child doing a poor job colouring between the lines. Her dress looked as though it had been through two spin cycles and was tie-dyed with what seemed like oil paint. Leaning closer, I saw that it was indeed alizarin crimson. We must have rolled over a tube and popped it open during one of our back-of-the-van episodes. My shirt too was covered with streaks of the bright red paint. Making matters perfectly clear to all, my fly was unzipped. And Priscilla's bra was askew, making her look as if she had an extra breast.

"Mummy, Daddy, darlings! Hello, Hello!" She made a rather ineffective effort to glide toward them at the far end of room, showering everyone with kisses and breathing fumes of the afternoon. Her father leaned forward in his chair and glared at me.

"Who's that?" he growled.

"That's Kerry, Daddy. He's ever so talented and he paints and he's ever so much fun and he was ever so kind and drove me down after the wedding. Isn't it swell?"

Daddy was unimpressed. "You drink port?" he growled again.

"Yes, sir!" Trying to be as respectful as possible.

"Give him a port."

With that settled, the group returned to its conversation. Our arrival clearly would have no consequence in the proceedings of their evening.

I was shown to my room, strategically located directly across the hall from Priscilla's. It was also right next to Mummy's and Daddy's. I was tired, exhausted in fact, so I excused myself, took a shower and crawled into bed with a cup of tea and a large bottle of aspirin.

I was awakened several hours later by Priscilla climbing in with me. I pleaded, saying I was much too exhausted. Besides, the Lord and Lady were next door on aristocratic alert. I knew they would be watchful lest the dreadful northern fellow make designs on their debutante. They were saving her for someone more — well, you know, suitable.

My earnest pleas went completely unheeded. She had spent her entire life getting precisely what she wanted, when she wanted it. The fact that Daddy would probably run me off with a shotgun if he discovered us didn't matter a whit to Priscilla. She had me pinned against the wall, inches away from Mummy and Daddy.

I must confess to enjoying what followed. There was something intensely erotic about having abandoned sex in a stately English manor house. Toying with disaster added spice to an already potent concoction.

As dawn glowed faintly through the window, Priscilla cooed her sweetnesses in my ear for what must have been the hundredth time within an eighteen-hour period. She took her leave, promising to bring me breakfast in bed. I lay still for ten or fifteen minutes after she crept out, giving her time to get back to her room and fall asleep, then quietly slipped out of bed and dressed. It was six o'clock and I was eager to get back to my own type of sanctuary at Earles Court.

As I crept down the stairs, I noticed that there were still paint streaks on my clothes and — sure enough — lipstick stains on my shirt. I was doing well, only a few yards from the front hallway. As I slid past the kitchen, I heard a movement.

"You'll take some tea."

It was Priscilla's mother, Lady Thing. What the hell was she doing up at this hour? I had been nabbed! I resigned myself to my fate and stepped into the kitchen.

"Oh, thank you. Good morning." I smiled with all the cheer I could muster. "Hope I didn't disturb anyone. I have to go back to London. Things to do, you know." I trailed off, hoping these words would somehow free me.

"Sugar?" The word was like the chiming of a large cracked bell. "Milk?" This was more like the clang of closing bars. "There are toast and preserves. We eat a light breakfast in the country."

The toast was cold, the butter was margarine, the preserves had gone to sugar, and the tea was like nothing I had ever tasted.

"From where do you hail?" She let a brief smile slide up one side of her face. Her eyes remained fixed and penetrating. "You work in some kind of artistic endeavour, I understand?"

"Oh, yes. In London."

"You have known my daughter long?"

"Well . . . not long, really. We have a mutual friend in television."

"Television, really . . . Yes. I suppose the masses must have some kind of recreation. I can't say that I approve. There's a lot of smut on TV these days."

"Don't watch that much myself," I said. "Never seem to have the time. Wimbledon and the Cup finals, that's about it." I laughed, hoping to ease the conversation into more casual gear.

"I used to play tennis as a girl," she continued with completely unbroken tension. "Nowadays it seems most anyone can play. They even have foreigners, I am told. Soccer of course is necessary to give the populace something to do on Saturdays. You didn't say where you were from?"

"Oh, sorry. I was born near Chesterfield. Derbyshire."

"Derbyshire, really. Then you must know the Duke and Duchess of Devonshire at Chatsworth."

Why not, I thought. Why the hell not? At this point, who cares? She deserves a kick up her aristocratic arse. "Oh, yes. I had their daughter in the stables one Sunday morning last autumn. Only they serve marmalade and coffee for breakfast."

14
Sketches in Sunlight

In most creative pursuits, the artist leads a precarious existence. We teeter on the brink of failure. We grapple with the prospect of falling below our expectations and remain in a continual state of siege with ourselves. We strive to capture an essence, a kernel, a definitive statement, a universal language. But it's a moving target. To hit it takes guile and cunning. You have to sneak up on it when its guard is down, when it least expects you, when it's doing the dishes.

There's risk involved.

Being creative can be hazardous to the health. Look at poor old Vincent.

Artists are invariably portrayed as thrift-shop derelicts. They're not to be trusted. One should never stand too close to them and never, ever let them within ten feet of your daughters.

This is a convenient and over-romanticized concept. But dealers and gallery owners feel more comfortable thinking this way. It gives them a head start. It's a lot easier to screw someone you regard as scum.

Artists are a pathetically vulnerable breed, always anxious to please, and willing to go to almost any length for that all-important pat on the back. It's little wonder that a lot of real talent has gone down the tubes.

Years ago, when I was a rather rancid young man with a spotty face and dark thoughts, I came to the conclusion that since I had been bathed in the sacred waters of Art College it would be foolish not to at least give it a try. It's taken thirty years or so to realize that I never really had a choice. I had been born with certain cards in my hand, and the only responsible course was to play them as dealt.

By the time I was eight, my father had become an invalid. The handsome, tall, natural athlete, who had played soccer for Liverpool and cricket for Derbyshire, spent his remaining years in an improvised bed-chair in front of the fire. He could move about a little, but the slightest exercise or excitement aggravated his condition.

Once I fell while playing on concrete steps and rushed home with blood on my forehead. One look at me and my father began gasping for air and clutching his chest. My poor mother had to administer to us both.

The injury left a thin scar on my forehead that is barely visible today. The emotional scars left by my father's reaction are even less visible, but undoubtedly deeper.

After that, Mother hardly allowed me to play out of sight of the house. She desperately wanted to prevent anything that would disturb my father. The result was that I spent long hours alone, either in my bedroom or, weather permitting, in the little garden behind our house. During this time I took solace in a new pastime, drawing and painting. Watercolours mostly, with some scribblings of pencil and pen and ink.

We didn't have money to spend on art materials, and my parents viewed such objects as little more than inanimate babysitters. But for me the long hours away from companions my own age were filled by drawing and painting. Watercolours were fun to produce. I enjoyed the challenge of making trees look like trees, hills look like hills, and water look like water. At that point, I suppose, art was nothing more than an exercise in visual deception. I had always been fascinated by magicians and card sharps, and painting had many of the same endearing qualities. The image of a lake at sunset was created by juggling patches of colour to produce the right combination of trickery and visual persuasion.

"Well, just look how he's got the ripples on the water!"

There were no ripples, no water. Merely a piece of inexpensive paper and an hour's work with a colour set and some old brushes. When I displayed my work, people usually got interested and gave me, physically or emotionally, the nurturing pat on the back I sought.

In the autumn of 1955, at the age of sixteen, I moved from the ivy-covered walls of high school to the pigeon-covered roofs of the local art college. I may have been a late bloomer, but no matter, I became consumed with an unquenchable appetite urging me to absorb anything and everything. Had it been possible, I would have slept at the art college. I was there from nine in the morning to ten in the evening every day except Saturday and Sunday. The staff needed a break, after all.

My days were filled with wonder, and that first year was one of the happiest I can recall. I felt exhilarated. For the first time, I felt that I was doing something of substance. I realized that, one way or another, art would be part of the tapestry of my life as far into the future as I could see — which at that time hardly extended beyond the following week.

While in my second year at art college and still living at home, I was dreaming of a career in art with little likelihood of being able to afford the necessary training. To embark on a full-scale art education, I needed to win the elusive Major Art Scholarship, offered by the Derbyshire County Council. This would allow me to continue my education in London at one of the finer universities.

The Derbyshire Council awarded only one scholarship each year. I had applied, and after months of intensive exams and presentations of paintings for "critical evaluation," I was informed that I was one of ten finalists. My entire future was in the hands of a committee, usually not the most enviable of circumstances.

One fine summer morning, I woke up and rushed downstairs to find a small brown envelope from the Education Department.

"We are pleased to inform you. . . ."

Mother was at work, which was fortunate because the sight of her son doing cartwheels down the front driveway in his pajamas might have put her off a bit. I decided that it would be better to tell her later, when I was a little more composed. But I decided to proceed immediately to a nearby restaurant to yell and scream with my mates.

It was a blazing blue summer morning as I walked down Crow Lane to town. The stroll gave me a chance to digest the news and muse about my future. Cuckoos carolled on the high elms, the hedgerows were warming in the sun, the edge of the wood was alive with birdsong, and cows munched at their cud, ignoring me as I passed.

Dashing into the wood, I stepped behind a large tree and took a celebratory pee. There's something about relieving one's self outdoors, in full sight of nature. Birds chirped and squirrels went about their business, paying me no mind whatsoever. And why should they? That morning I was as natural as they, on the road at last to fulfilling my destiny.

I must say it was one of the best leaks I've ever had.

Early September, golden and lovely. Rooks were squawking in the high poplars. The sun was still low behind the ruined castle where I had played when a child. It would be an exceptional day.

I hadn't slept well the night before. I was far too exited. Moving to London was a big deal, a very big deal. It meant being able to come and go as I pleased, to have the freedom to stretch and explore.

Studying painting in London with the big boys would be a lot different from the time I had spent at art college in Chesterfield. The University of London Central School of Arts and Crafts was larger, the staff a good deal more imposing, and the atmosphere considerably less intimate. There were departments such as metalworking and photography that until then I had never considered remotely artistic.

Quite a few of my new professors were practicing artists, and a few were enjoying real success. My drawing professor had work hanging in the Tate Gallery, and a couple of my painting teachers were showing at prestigious galleries around London.

I had packed, unpacked, and repacked numerous times. Ready for wearing were my favorite pair of ultra-tight jeans, a seaman's sweater with rolled collar, and the mandatory art student's duffle coat. With these on I not only was an art student on the way to London, I looked like one. I imagined people stopping and staring, saying, "There goes Kerry Hallam, the art student, on his way to London."

Mother had been up for hours busying herself with all kinds of bits and bobs. Until the last moment she found a hundred tasks to keep her busy — dusting, polishing, moving a chair here or there, washing the same cup for the tenth time.

"Well, you'd best be off then or you'll miss your bus," she finally said.

I tried to pretend that I hadn't noticed the time.

"Mind you stay out of pubs and get enough to eat — and don't forget to write. I'll be up here worrying myself silly. But I don't count anymore, I know."

That was as close as we were going to get to a bon voyage, so I decided to depart with as little show of emotion as possible. It was, after all, how she seemed to want it.

Kissing her on the cheek and telling her not to worry, I turned at the gate, waved, and walked down the road to the bus stop. I was trembling a little, my eyes beginning to moisten. I felt terrible leaving Mother alone. Most of all, I was saddened by the stoic northern disposition that is so terrified of showing emotion.

The old green- and cream-coloured bus came round the corner, and I stood waiting for it with the other passengers. I caught a glimpse of Mother waving from the back porch. I waved one last time to her and started boarding.

The bus plodded wearily past my old primary school, where kids gaggled on the playground.

It wove its way past the churchyard, where I once kissed Katie Stokes on a moist October evening after choir practice.

Past the cricket field, flat as a billiard table, where my dad used to play before he took ill.

Through the village, where the grocer was just opening and the butcher was late as usual. I noticed Mr. Thompson setting out on the morning run with his horse and milk dray.

The trip took me down eighteen years of memories, and as the bus finally pulled into the railway station, I gazed back from where we had come. The mist had burnt off, and it was a clear warm morning. I had never seen Hady Lane look so beautiful.

I wasn't sure if my leaving deserved a goodbye or an au revoir. Turned out it was a goodbye. We can never go back.

The train arrived and my colleagues and I climbed aboard. Slowly the huge locomotive edged its way out of the station, picking up speed over the points at Horns Bridge.

I gazed back at the receding town and settled into the seat. Better take one last look, I thought. I'm only going to do this once in my life.

15

Return to Ramatuelle

The winter that I returned to London from the south of France was raw and unrelenting. But then, most winters in London are. The English have never accepted that there are four seasons, preferring to maintain that there is only one season throughout the Isles: an ongoing twelve months of picture-perfect mildness without temperature or precipitation changes.

English apparel reflects this. The same men's suit is often worn year round, adding perhaps a topcoat when an Arctic blizzard descends in January, or removing a scarf at Wimbledon in July when court temperatures hover around a hundred. For ladies, tweed skirt and jacket are mandatory regardless of season.

This remarkable reluctance to acknowledge the shifts in climate also manifests in architecture. Double glazing was an unspeakable luxury until recent years. Insulation? Now really. Storm doors? Excuse me? Central heating? Unhealthy and expensive. Air conditioning? Inconceivable.

Underlying this thinking is the old Victorian doctrine of needing to suffer to be considered truly British. In those dim and distant days, when our predecessors were systematically colonizing the globe with God on their side, they needed to set an example. Waste not want not, a penny saved is a penny earned, stiff upper lip and all that sort of thing.

When I arrived back in London near the end of November, the oncoming Christmas season kept my spirits high. But January and February were interminable. By the middle of March, I was ready to pack it in.

One frigid evening near the end of the month, I arrived for my stint at a basement club in which I had been playing. As I descended the cellar steps, I heard the sounds of a guitar and a woman's voice. The guitar work was superb. The voice sounded professional and strong. I had a catch in my throat even before the club's owner saw me.

"Oh — yes — well, we decided to make a change," he said when I asked what was going on.

"Where's that leave me?"

"You can come in and listen, if you like. But I'll have to charge you admission. Ten bob." He smiled and turned his attention to some customers just walking in.

"Hang on a bit," I said. "You're telling me that I have to pay to get in? I'm supposed to be the entertainment!"

His smile faded, and a rather stony look came into his eyes.

"Not any more, mate. You follow?"

The new singer, a beautiful girl named Ruth, was an American studying sculpture in London. As it turned out, she was a much better folk musician than I. She deserved the gig.

As a matter of principle, I refused to give my ex-employer the satisfaction of seeing me fork over ten bob to drink his watered-down swill. (No bitterness here, you'll notice.)

At closing time I waited outside to introduce myself to Ruth. She was apologetic and assured me that she had not known the situation when the owner of the club engaged her. As we walked, I noticed that she shivered in the night air. Slender and graceful, she said that the cold had always gone right through her. We sat and chatted at a small coffee bar around the corner from the club. It turned out that she had been hoping to visit the south of France in the spring to do some drawing and painting. When I told her about my studio and the village, she thought it sounded charming. It was just the kind of thing that she had hoped to find. The evening ended, and I walked her to her bedsitter on Earles Court Road.

The next few days we saw quite a bit of each other, and on one visit to her room played our guitars and sang together. She was more accomplished on the guitar than I, and her voice stronger, but we harmonized well.

It was the end of March. I had been in England for nearly four months, and my funds were gone. London had the post-winter blues. Drizzling rain fell day after soggy day. The sun never seemed to break through, and everyone was waiting for the first signs of spring.

Anika and Maggie, my two friends from the beach club in St. Tropez, had arrived back in London about the same time as I. They were by now eager to return to the warmth and sunshine of the Côte d'Azur. They suggested that the three of us join up with Ruth and use my old van to get back to Ramatuelle, splitting petrol and expenses. After all, I had my studio and could certainly accommodate three more for a time.

I called the eccentric owner of my house in Ramatuelle. She assured me that she would be delighted to rent me the wine cellar, much the same as the previous summer. She assured me that she had stored my art gear in the studio, and everything would be ready at my arrival.

It didn't take long to make plans. Ruth seemed delighted. Although she was having success in the London club scene, it wasn't a straightforward situation for her. She was an American without working papers in England and had to be paid under the table. Besides, she wanted to get back to her sculpting and painting.

Within a week, Ruth, Anika, Maggie, and I were crammed into the minivan, heading for France with piles of luggage strapped on top. Not one of us had much we were leaving behind. Four nomads at sail, it seemed. Perhaps it was the times, or our age. We gave it not a thought as we drove off.

It was an exhausting trip. We felt like sardines by the time we arrived in the village. Maggie and Anika both had colds verging on the flu. We badly needed the luxury of a hot bath, food, and sleep.

Arriving in my lovely village, I parked the girls in the café whilst I hauled luggage down to the studio.

A bright shiny new lock was on the door. I put down the

luggage and took out my key. Despite all my hopes, it would not fit the lock. I stood outside my own studio, helpless and frustrated.

After half an hour or so, I managed to contact the owner of the house by phone.

"Well, you see," she said, "I was obliged to rent it to the post lady. I mean, I had to have some rent. You do understand, don't you? Where are you now?"

I told her that I was in the post office calling from a phone booth.

"I'm sure you'll be able to find something just as suitable," she said. "Must fly now, I'm painting a model and she's only here for another half hour."

With that, she hung up. For long moments I stood with the receiver still in my hand. I realized that I had not asked about my painting supplies, which she had been storing in the studio.

I would address that soon enough. First I had to break the news to the ladies. Returning to the café, I saw that they were in fine form, all the better for several glasses of wine. Their spirits were high, and I was welcomed as a returning hero.

It took only a few seconds for the mood to take an acute 180-degree turn. What did I mean — rented? To whom? Had I bothered to check with the landlady? Was the studio a figment of my imagination? Was I a congenital idiot as well as liar?

It was clearly time to make a new plan.

16
The Cabenon

Marie Ange, bless her cotton socks, had a small *cabenon* in her vineyard which was used by workers in September at *vendange*, grape-picking time. It was April now, and she agreed to rent it to us until it was needed. Not having anything else, we agreed to take a look. If it proved suitable, it would at least help get me out of the dog house with the three ladies.

The small cabenon was charmingly attractive from the exterior, but starkly primitive inside. It stood isolated in an extensive field of grape vines. Row after neat row of dark umber roots writhed in anticipation of the warm weather soon to arrive.

The cabenon had two rooms, one with a pair of rumpled, beaten-down double beds. The other had a large wood stove and a rough dining table with four chairs. A few pots and pans and a big metal iron sat on the stove. Opening a drawer, we saw assorted pieces of ancient cutlery, most of which weren't too badly rusted.

Each room had one window, with shutters badly in need of paint. There was no bathroom, no electricity. Immediately outside the front door was a well with a bucket to lower for water. The cabenon was at least watertight, which would make it comfortable during the hard French spring rains. It did have the fundamentals to support life.

We decided to take it — as if we had an option. First things first: we needed sheets and blankets, provisions and candles. One trip back to the village got us most of the things we needed. A few hours later, we were sitting down to a yellow-pepper omelette, fresh bread, and wine. It was a delicious, life-changing kind of meal. Ruth and I sang a few songs after dinner, and the evening passed in the pleasant warmth of the wood stove and candles. We were all drowsy. It had been a long day. The rather delicate problem of who would sleep with whom was resolved by Anika proclaiming that she and I would sleep in one bed, Ruth and Maggie in the other.

"And mark you," Anika said, looking straight at me, "I don't want any funny stuff."

I was by this time completely infatuated with Anika. She was lovely and desirable. All the way down from London I had searched for an appropriate occasion to let her know that I had escalated from chum to *amoureuse*, but no such chance had come along. Consequently, she had no idea of my feelings.

I knew that sleeping in the same bed was going to be frustrating. Fortunately, exhaustion and wine overtook us and we both fell asleep within moments.

Next morning, the sky was clear. The sun warmed the little cabenon and tickled the sleeping *cigalons* into their rattling chorale. A clump of trees became our designated bathroom, and we all did our best with a bucket of water and a spade.

Sitting on the grassy knoll outside the kitchen, we breakfasted on toast and coffee. The feeling of contentment was short lived. Abruptly, almost at the same moment, we all realized that we were broke and miles from the nearest village. We had one old minivan between us — and no prospects of employment.

As always, Anika met the problem head on. Maggie and she would try to get their jobs back at the beach club. The club wasn't open yet, but certainly there would be work available for experienced people who could help get everything ready. They also would try to find a place for Ruth. As for me, well . . . Yes, "Well indeed."

Without my studio, the thought of the summer tourist season seemed bleak. Paintings on the Port again. Running the gauntlet with the police. Not a pleasant thought.

17
Busking

That evening, our friends Peter and Stewart invited us to dine with them at the house they were renovating. An Englishman had bought it as an absolute ruin and had retained them to refurbish it in French provincial. They had been hard at work for the last two months, and were starved for English company. More to the point, they had not been close to a woman since moving to the village, and they were eager for us to visit. Wine flowed, and after dinner Ruth and I serenaded the group. Under the influence of the wine and general bonhomie, we sounded quite good.

"Well, that's one problem solved," Peter said after the third song.

I took a sip of wine and looked at him blankly, not understanding what he meant.

"Off you both go to St. Tropez and hit a few restaurants," he explained. "Pass the hat round after you sing and you'll make a fortune."

"You're joking," I said. "We're not good enough."

"Sure you are. And anyway, who cares? They'll be eating and drinking and it'll drown out any mistakes. Just keep smiling!"

Everyone else agreed that this was a great idea, although

Ruth and I had far less confidence. But then it sank in a bit. I realized that her professional air would carry us through any situation, and besides, we had little choice.

Next day we rehearsed our three songs, and by late afternoon had the words and chords down. Our voices did seem to harmonize well. I had a certain gruffness (I like to say character) in my voice. And Ruth sang like an angel. We began to feel a little more secure.

By seven o'clock we were ready. Wearing the closest to our Sunday best, we drove down to St. Tropez. The town was quiet; the season was a long way off, but a few restaurants were busy. With confidence born of terror we approached the patron of a likely looking spot. In halting French, I asked if we might sing a few songs and *fait le casket* (pass the hat). He probably would have been more excited if we'd volunteered to swat flies for him in the kitchen. But he agreed, saying no harm could be done. After all, he himself wouldn't be paying us.

After that, there was no way out. We were committed. My hands shook and I had butterflies. Ruth was used to it. She had sung in restaurants in the States, earning extra money since high school. She assured me that no singer had ever been lynched by an angry mob of diners, so. . . .

We wandered out unannounced, just standing in the large room with people eating all around us. Gulping and taking a deep breath, we started singing "Blowing in the Wind".

I was astonished. We sounded quite good. Certainly we didn't seem out of place. I glanced over at the patron's face between verses and could tell that he wasn't displeased. When we finished, we received polite applause from the room.

We followed with "It Ain't Me Babe". Then the grande finale, "Homeward Bound". The ordeal was over. I collapsed into a corner and put our guitars into their cases whilst Ruth took round the wicker basket.

Nineteen francs had never looked so good!

My apprehensions dissolved as we hotfooted it to Senequiers for coffee. The crazy idea had worked. The sudden swing of fortune left me lightheaded, and we drove back to the cabenon in high spirits.

Maggie and Anika had found jobs in St. Tropez. They were set, and it seemed that Ruth and I had solved our problems.

What a difference a day makes.

During the next few weeks, Ruth and I consolidated our "spots." We pinpointed eight restaurants at which we could sing on any given evening. We could play at only three or four during prime time, but the others provided insurance in case one or two were light on customers. We quickly picked up the knack of assessing the size and affluence of the crowd in a particular restaurant before committing ourselves. This was very important. A correct evaluation, we found, was directly proportional to the size of our take.

The customers enjoyed our singing. Even the patrons began taking to us. Their demeanor changed from indifference to mild cordiality.

Other problems, more personal, continued to distract me. Sleeping in the same bed with the ravishing Anika was getting depressing. Then out of nowhere she announced that she was thinking of going to Aix-en-Provence with a family that needed a bilingual nanny. She woke up a few mornings later and packed, leaving with but a brief good-bye.

I was dejected and forlorn. Maggie and Ruth were initially sympathetic, but after a few days my grumpy silence got on their nerves. The three of us were about to move into a rather spacious apartment on Rue D'Eglise in St. Tropez, and they intimated that they would prefer not to have a whining, star-crossed lover as a roommate. I took a hard look at myself in the mirror and put it behind me.

We made the move to our new quarters, which were much more in the direction of palatial than any of us could have imagined a month earlier. We bid farewell to the cabenon, returning Marie Ange's sheets and blankets. The well outside the door, the musty walls, and the outdoor loo would not be missed.

Ruth and I were becoming well set among the restaurants of St. Tropez's expensive Port area, which wined and dined the wealthy and famous of four continents. Our repertoire was expanding. Every day we learned a few more songs, and our guitar work and harmonies were becoming more inventive.

Things were happening. We were being sought out for engagements. Restaurant customers would remember us when planning special events. They would approach us between songs, asking if we could entertain aboard their yacht for the weekend, or at their villa for a party. It was a wonderful way to make a living. We felt free and were making good, steady money. Best of all, it was cash-hard, sweet, and put directly into our pockets. The French bureaucratic system, despite itself, worked to our advantage. Neither Ruth nor I had formal working papers, but we were protected from awkward enquiries — provided that we remained inside the restaurants.

There is tacit agreement in France that patrons (owners) of cafés, bars, and restaurants should be allowed to conduct their affairs without official moderation. Once a restaurateur has run the gamut of red tape and has fulfilled all requirements to open a restaurant, the authorities have little interest in what goes on inside.

By June, when the Season proper kicked in, we were singing at two beach clubs during lunch hours and three of the most expensive and popular restaurants in the evening. This gave us an average take of around 300 francs per day, more than enough to equip us with new clothing, toiletries, and servicing for my long-suffering minivan.

Our professional life was building. We were considered cute, charming, *mignon*. That we sang only in English was a fascination, and a boy/girl duet was unique at the time. Ruth was strikingly beautiful — elfin, slim, and graceful with a commanding stage presence. She had a riveting voice and accompanied herself with exceptional guitar work. I provided the perfect foil, the necessary accouterment for the perception of innocent romance. We were pure and aesthetic, in contrast to the jaded, world-weary jet set of the mid-60s that made up much of the clientele in the finer St. Tropez restaurants and clubs.

Throughout all this, our art took a back seat, although we refused to give it up entirely. We considered our careers in music to be nothing more than temporary. Ruth had come to Europe to study sculpture, and I still judged everything that befell me by the artistic compass in my heart. We sketched daily, and I made a point of standing at my easel for an hour each morning before leaving to serenade the St. Tropez lunch crowd.

How to back away from success? At that point, we simply

could not. Our engagements for private parties and social functions increased. Soon, we were singing almost every weekend on a fabulous yacht with waves lapping lazily around us. The food was free (usually catered and out of this world), the pay was outstanding, and it was liberating for the spirit simply to be around the rich and debauched.

We were artists on a detour.

18

Bridgette Bardot and Friends

One afternoon as I was walking through St. Tropez, a man hailed me from a passing car. He told me that he was an assistant to Bridgette Bardot, who was vacationing in the area. Apparently he had seen us perform several times and enjoyed our act tremendously. He informed me that his employer would be dining with friends at Chez Ferdinand that evening. Perhaps we would like to drop by and sing a few songs?

Yes, we most certainly would.

Ruth and I showed up early and sang an entire set before Mademoiselle Bardot arrived. When she came in, accompanied by her entourage, the atmosphere of the entire restaurant tangibly changed. Before, people had been themselves — that is to say, noisy and somewhat overanxious to get each forkful into their mouths. With her entrance, everything became like a movie set. Everyone, almost at the same moment, sat up straighter and began eating more delicately. Such was the effect of her presence in the room. It was as though cameras were rolling.

With her were Johnny Halliday, the internationally famous French recording artist, Eddie Vatin, a well-known record producer, and Christine Deneuve, Catherine Deneuve's sister. Mlle. Bardot had not yet met Gunther Sachs, and she was with several gentlemen we did not know. Eleven or twelve in all, the group took up the large central table.

Mlle. Bardot liked Chez Ferdinand, I'm sure, because it was up in the village away from the crowds. I can imagine how difficult it would have been for her to dine in The Port. She was quite relaxed, alarmingly beautiful, and was absolutely the center of attention at every moment.

We started singing, and I can assure you my knees were shaking. But suddenly everyone in the restaurant was attentive to our music. Instead of talking and slurping down food over our singing, as they had done only moments before, they were suddenly on their best behavior. They must have thought that because Bridgette Bardot was in the room, we had been approved by her.

Our set went without a hitch, and afterward we had a gratifying surprise. We were accustomed to passing a hat, and we had quite an unusual one to pass: a big felt top hat. It was always a conversation piece. Ruth passed it at one table off to the right of the stage, then went to Mlle. Bardot's table. As Ruth approached, Mlle. Bardot stood up, took the hat and passed it round the table herself.

The bottom of that top hat was very rigid, and you could always hear a plunk whenever a coin was dropped in. When Mlle. Bardot passed it, we heard nothing but folding money.

Ruth took it round the rest of the room. As though we had been "approved," everyone threw in very silent bills. You couldn't hear a centime drop. What a fabulous evening!

The following week, Ruth and I made *Elle* magazine, full page, with a photo and reportage of "the new singing sensation of St. Tropez." Our local reputation, already solid, was established. The patrons loved to see us coming. We found ourselves sorting out invitations, deciding which to accept and which to decline.

19
Salvador Dali's Birthday

Our good friend Mr. Fernand was patron of one of the most elegant St. Tropez restaurants. Still in his thirties, he had taken a nondescript café at the edge of the fashionable area and in only a few years had created an establishment where every night the rich and famous could dine in the discreet comfort of his spacious terrace, or in the even more discreet "interior." The aroma of steak and lemon-basted fish wafted from his grill, and white-jacketed waiters floated between tables in their mime dance of servitude.

Ruth and I would take up our positions and sing three or four songs, after which we would pass through the tables with our top hat, collecting tips. Half an hour later we might sing a few more songs, then again pass through the crowd. At the end of the evening we would change small bills for large ones. This helped Fernand with his change, and underscored the weight of our take, which on a good night was substantial. This exchange was usually accompanied by a glass of wine, a brief chat, and his thanks to us for gracing his establishment.

One evening, Mr. Fernand asked if we would sing for a private party *dans l'interior*. He said that he himself would *fait le casket*. In other words, he would pay us as much as we would expect to make from passing the hat. He insisted that we not accept tips from the table.

81

Since we had never visited his private sacristy, let alone sang in it, we assured him that we would be delighted to oblige. We were ushered into an exceptionally elegant provencal dining room. Dimly lighted, it had the beautifully understated decor and atmosphere of a wealthy private home.

At a long wooden table, a dozen or so diners were attacking their meals with great seriousness. At the center of the table sat Salvador Dali, instantly recognizable. Ruth and I were stunned.

Despite our recent induction into the world of the jet set (singing to oil barons and international arms dealers), we were still capable of embarrassment. After all, there in front of us was one of the icons of the art world. But we slowly regained our composure and presented our songs.

The table was quietly appreciative. Most diners continued to eat as we played. We bowed and prepared to leave.

The gentleman sitting next to Mr. Dali rose and moved around the table toward us, still chewing and dabbing his lips with his napkin. In French he asked if Madame, meaning Ruth, would care to have Mr. Dali sign the front of her guitar. Apparently Mr. Dali felt that she was exquisitely beautiful and sang like an angel.

I smiled and thanked him, quickly translating for Ruth.

"Not bloody likely," she said. "It's a handmade Favilla. No one scratches the varnish-it would ruin the sound board!"

"Christ, we could sell it and buy ten more!" I whispered in English. Ruth was unconvinced.

With as much levity and as diplomatically as my halting French would allow, I translated Ruth's reply. Clearly upset, the gentleman leaned over and dutifully whispered to his boss.

Mr. Dali listened for a moment, then burst into a belly laugh, spilling his wine and spraying the table with pieces of half-chewed steak. He asked that two chairs be inserted next to him and insisted that we join the table for dessert and coffee.

"I like people who know what they want," he said.

We spent the next hour eating *tart au citron* and luxuriating in coffee, cognac, and the heady ambrosia of fame and fortune.

Life really was thrilling.

20

Two For The Road

The coastline of Southern France, with its rolling hills and luxurious villas overlooking the Mediterranean, is among the most beautiful and romantic in the world. While we were there, a film of some sort was always being shot in or around the area. Most have been relegated to bleak storerooms in abandoned warehouses, where stray cats straggle in to die. But I can recall two that survived.

The film that put St. Tropez on the map was one of Mlle. Bardot's first. Made in the fifties, *The Light Across the Street* was a moderately good piece of work that unleashed the awesome power of Bardot's earthy French sexuality. With the success of the film, and others that followed, she became a link between screen sirens of classic days (Gish, Harlow, Deitrich, etc.) and our contemporaries.

Delighted with the atmospheric allure of the area, Mlle. Bardot settled in St. Tropez. Those who could afford it (and find it) followed. Certain areas of the world, even with their unique charm, need a jump start to become famous.

The other film of note made in the area was *Two for the Road*, directed by Stanley Donen and starring Audrey Hepburn and Albert Finney. A box-office hit worldwide, the film featured Ruth and myself as local singers. I use the word "featured" rather loosely. We can be spotted by a careful viewer, unless the eyes blink during the moments we're onscreen. Our parts might have been more substantial, but such is fate.

At the time, we were singing in three different restaurants every night. It was inevitable that we would be present during filming of one or another of the local movies. In this case, the casting director of *Two for the Road*, a rather nervous woman who was either smoking or biting her nails, saw us perform and decided that we would be a nice touch as background in one of their shots.

We were invited to her table and agreed to launch our movie careers the following morning. Our job was to provide the musical backdrop for a restaurant scene on the beach. We arrived in my decrepit orange minivan, which by that time was much in need of dignified retirement. It still served as reliable transportation, but was strikingly incongruous beside the shining rows of Mercedes, Jaguars, Rolls Royces, and Ferraris.

This was the first feature film set I had seen. The atmosphere was exhilarating, filled with electrical intensity. Trailers, vans, lights, and wiring seemed to extend for miles across the beach. Technicians huddled in groups, making what seemed like life-and-death decisions. Three separate camera crews waited patiently, ready to film from different angles. The director, Stanley Donen, was consulting with Mr. Finney and Ms. Hepburn. The two stars were like the hub of a giant wheel. Everything revolved around them. Everything focused on them and awaited their readiness.

Ruth and I waited for well over an hour after arriving. Finally, the casting director arrived and showed us to the set. The make-up crew gave us a quick once-over. They looked at Ruth and declared us simply stunning and ready to be filmed.

The scene was arranged, rearranged, then rearranged again. Tables were reset and reset again. Fresh fruit was exchanged for fresher fruit. Table cloths, already looking perfectly smooth and starched, were taken off to be re-ironed. Furniture was polished and repolished, reflector shells put in place, tracking rails adjusted, sand smoothed, the extras briefed and given positions — on and on and on.

After about three hours of this intense preparation, all was ready. Ms. Hepburn floated from her trailer onto the set. Mr. Finney followed a few minutes later. After a brief consultation with the director, they were ready for a practice run.

Given the prearranged signal, we launched into our first song.

Cut! Cut! Cut!

Stanley Donen was incensed. "What on earth is going on? Doesn't anyone listen? Try it again. Quickly! And oh yes — some other song. Something romantic."

After twenty or so attempts at finding a song that satisfied him, our repertoire was exhausted. Mr. Donen mentioned, rather late in the game, I thought, that American folk music was not exactly what he had envisioned for the scene. Someone suggested that since this was a French café, shouldn't the singing be in French? This concept apparently had not crossed the minds of the people who had hired us. The casting lady was sulking, and we were feeling decidedly like fish out of water. It was getting to the point that the entire day's shooting could be washed out simply because we were wrong for the scene.

After a hurried consultation, it was decided that we should pretend to sing and play. Sound editors would later dub in the voices of a French couple. Our movie debut consisted of performing songs with our mouths moving and our fingers plucking, with no sound issuing from either.

We were paid, however, and agreed to come back next day for more of the same. The following morning was spent waiting. Lunch arrived, and still there had been no shooting. Mr. Finney was having a great time with the extras on the beach. He was a pleasant person who seemed unaffected by his star status. He and I chatted for a while about growing up in the north of England. Our backgrounds were similar, and he wished us well with our plans.

Ms. Hepburn, a lady of great style and class, was in her trailer throughout the long wait. Apparently, it was understood that in no case would she ever come out until everything was ready to roll.

The powers-that-be had decided to shoot the final scene of the picture, in which Mr. Finney and Ms. Hepburn drive up to a customs barrier in an immaculate white Mercedes coupe. Everything was ready to roll, when from high on his scaffold, which towered at least fifty feet above the ground, Mr. Donen shouted down with his megaphone. He wanted another vehicle to follow immediately behind the Mercedes — to add a touch of realism perhaps.

My old orange minivan was at the head of the line of parked cars. The frazzled casting lady rushed over and told us to pull up behind the Mercedes as quickly as we could.

"Are you quite sure it's suitable?" I asked.

"Quick! Do it, please." Her teeth were clenched. "Don't ask any more questions."

I shrugged and pulled forward, slamming to a halt behind a rather alarmed Mr. Finney and Ms. Hepburn. They looked back at Ruth and me, then at each other. Shrugging, they took their positions for the shot.

Everything was set. Cameras were poised. Suddenly, from his perch on high, Mr. Donen let out a tirade.

"You call that a car? Get that goddamned thing out of here! Christ Almighty!"

My minivan was immune to insult by now. We reversed as quietly and discreetly as we could, but swerved a little and accidentally backed into Mr. Donen's scaffold. It wobbled a bit, but seemed quite sturdy. No harm done, I figured.

But at a fifty-foot height, even a mild wobble becomes intensified. As Ruth and I hit the tower, Mr. Donen and assistants screamed in terror, clutching the hand rails as though the whole scaffold was toppling. After long moments, another stream of abuse was hurled through the bullhorn in our general direction. We were finally led back to the safety of the other vehicles.

"Not a bad day's work!" I said, lighting a cigarette with the whole of filmdom looking at us, wondering what rock we had crawled out from under.

I felt that I had all the ingredients. The intangibles that mysteriously collect and form a whole greater than the sum of the parts. I could have become another McQueen, Redford, or Newman. But the film crew of *Two for the Road* had no vision. Great careers get snuffed out in this fashion.

We were paid for the day and told that our services would no longer be required. They will never know what they missed.

21
Peacocks

David Hamilton, ageless and debonair, the now world-renowned photographer of the pubescent female landscape, introduced us one evening to Monsieur and Madame Thiroux de Chalamanoux. These renowned lovers of the unusual were exceptionally aristocratic, having inherited half the hillside overlooking the village. They seemed very friendly — if a little odd.

Ruth, who had developed a few choice French phrases almost completely without accent, and I, with my engaging English grunts and gestures, were invited to their chateau for dinner. On the drive up the mountain, Ruth was puzzled and concerned. She was convinced that she kept seeing fleeting, glistening rainbows in the brush alongside the road. Ghosts? Hallucinations? If so, we were hallucinating together, for I started seeing the same shimmering wisps.

As we entered the chateau driveway, we encountered dozens of peacocks strutting freely, parading their exquisite plumes. Entire battalions scurried around the grounds.

The chateau had once been magnificent. Now it was in complete disrepair at the hands of this excessively wealthy and decidedly eccentric couple. The peacocks had taken control. At least they thought they had. Wandering at will around the property, one or another of them made an alarming strangulated cry every few minutes. Whenever one of them let fly, chills ran up my spine.

Sexual to-and-froing? Territorial imperative? Rising of the moon? I don't know why they issued such an unearthly squawk, but they continued their eerie crowing throughout the evening.

Peacocks are the oddest of creatures when they think they have the upper hand on you. They gather, swarming, and watch you closely. "You're in our territory," they seem to say. They never actually attack, but standing in their presence on those bizarre grounds, I could believe such a thing happening.

It's difficult to imagine the size of their droppings — or the odour. Large piles of the stuff were left untouched all about the yard. Taking a simple stroll through the roses was like walking through a mine field. Our hosts were oblivious. They had developed an instinct for stepping in the right places. Ruth and I checked our shoes every few steps.

Drinks were served on the terrace. After several attempts to find a seat not covered with dirt or dung, Ruth and I remained standing. The glasses were smoky, with a thin film of grease. The wine was of a quality I had seldom tasted.

Pandemonium broke out at the far end of the terrace as a gaggle of peacocks got into a family dispute. Our host let out a torrent of abusive French and hurled his glass with its contents in their general direction. The peacocks screeched off into the bushes.

Dinner was served in the interior. With not a servant to be seen, our aristocratic and immensely wealthy hosts slid piles of newspapers, magazines, books, and the remnants of a previous meal to one end of the table. They managed to clear four chairs. As far as I could tell, this room was peacock free. The dust and debris made up for it, along with the odour wafting in from the lawns.

Our host and hostess happily rambled on about this and that, until the lady excused herself to set the table and bring in dinner. The crockery and tableware were exquisite, simply the best that money could buy. All were covered with a thin layer of dust, grime, or peacock droppings.

The food was tasty and the wine out of this world. I could picture local retailers rubbing their hands in delight at the arrival of this rich, completely daft twosome.

We took cognac and coffee with the peacocks on the far terrace.

"Really a delicious meal," I said. "I don't think I've ever had chicken that good."

Our hosts exchanged furtive glances. After a long pause, the lady turned and fixed me with a smile.

"Monsieur Kerry, that was not chicken."

We left the chateau to the plaintive cackle of a peacock chorus. We had promised to return, but the words rang hollow as they fell from our mouths.

Several weeks later I saw the couple in a market, buying wine, vegetables, and bread.

But no meat. In that department they were well supplied.

22

Colours of Autumn

Wehad done our best to continue sketching and painting, but more and more it fell away. I woke up one Sunday morning and realized that I hadn't touched a paintbrush in over two weeks. Enough was enough. Ruth and I agreed to take some time off, perhaps get away to sketch in the countryside.

We decided to drive and take a few days off, stay a few nights in a fine hotel, and return within the week. We resolved even to leave our guitars behind. A vacation, we felt, would force us to forget music for awhile and concentrate on our first loves.

By that time, we had replaced my broken-down minivan with a Renault Quatre 'L. Just before we were scheduled to shove off, the alternator stopped alternating. There was no place to repair it locally, so we started anyway. We headed east along the Riviera, then cut north, planning to stop in Grasse to have the car repaired.

It turned out that we couldn't take the car above ten or fifteen miles an hour on the open road. It simply wouldn't go any faster, even with the pedal to the floor. But at that ridiculously slow speed we really had the chance to take in the feel of the countryside. Driving so slowly, we savored every mile of the journey.

We first travelled up through "Lavender Country," which was in full bloom. What a magnificent part of the world! Acre after acre of gorgeous lavender. Most of the large perfume manufacturers owned land in the area, using it to grow their precious scents. Southern France is a magical atmosphere for an artist. We passed near St. Remy and Arles, where Van Gogh stalked landscapes; Antibes, where Picasso painted tucked away in his mansion; Nice, Matisse's backyard; Cagnes, site of Renoir's gardens and olive forest; and Aix-En-Provence, where Cezanne's studio and garden had been turned into a national museum.

Travelling in this region is like sojourning in the inner sanctum of "Impressionism and Twentieth Century Art." We stopped late morning and unloaded our watercolour gear. Working side by side, we painted a view of ripe yellow fields stretching to blue mountains in the distance. By the time we looked up, the afternoon was well gone. Putting our easels away, we devoured cream cheese sandwiches and a bottle of wine before getting back into the car.

That afternoon we bought two lavender bouquets for about the equivalent of a quarter. Every petal eventually fell to the floor, giving the car the smell of a sachet.

During the rest of our first day out, the journey north was delightful. Driving slowly, savoring each passing sight, we worked our way higher and higher into the mountains. Afternoon turned to evening and evening to night.

All at once we needed a place to stay, but as miles passed, we saw nothing resembling an hotel. It got quite dark and late. I was more than a little apprehensive. We were both tired, and I had not planned on our sleeping in the car.

On a particularly deserted stretch, we spotted a light in the distance. Sure enough, as we drew close it showed every sign of being an hotel. Pulling into the rather luxurious drive, I rushed inside to the concierge.

"*Bonsoir, madame. Avez vous un chambre pour ce soir?*"

"*Oui, Monsier,*" she said, smiling.

I didn't even bother asking the price. I signed the card as quickly as I could before someone else grabbed the room. A porter helped us with our things up the elevator. I wasn't expecting it to be much. We were, after all, exactly halfway to the middle of nowhere.

The porter showed us to an utterly charming suite with exquisite decor and every appointment. The building had been constructed in the old style. Its conversion to a hotel had been accomplished with taste and preservation of character.

I asked the gentleman if it would be possible to get a sandwich. I said I realised it was late, but we had been travelling all day.

"There is a restaurant downstairs, monsieur," he said in perfect English. "It's open until eleven."

I thanked him, and we quickly dumped our baggage. Hurrying down, we figured that it would no doubt be the equivalent of fish and chips. We didn't care, as long as it supplied some sort of nourishment.

We entered a stately, wood-panelled dining room with waiters in tuxedos scurrying among fifteen very full and animated tables. Where in the world had all the people come from? The odours of the food and the sight of the platters made my mouth water. We were quickly seated, with wine orders taken.

It was a meal I remember as though we sat down to it yesterday. Fresh local salad with a basil vinaigrette. Sauteed shrimp with tangerines and tamarind. Filet mignon that we cut with our forks, served with new potatoes, vegetables, and a sauce made in heaven. A creme caramel. Cheeses and coffee. The wine was a Bordeaux, the cognac and coffee excellent.

We slept like babes.

Next morning, we breakfasted on fresh croissants and coffee on a little terrace off our room. The view of the mountain crests could not have been improved if ordered by mail.

The hotel was named "La Diligence." The bill came to sixty francs. I have the receipt framed on my wall.

Such are the unexpected joys of travel.

23

Recording Executives

When we arrived back in St. Tropez, the whirlwind began all over. Our fifteen minutes of semi-fame had arrived full tilt. We were ushered from one event to the next in a frenzy. Yachting parties, private dinners at dazzling villas, libations at five by luxurious swimming pools — the atmosphere and sometimes daft circumstances surrounding flamboyant wealth had to be dealt with.

It became fashionable among the wealthy to include us in any kind of social event. As the season progressed, we were able to pick and choose when and where we wanted to play. We kept the three best restaurants as insurance and let the others go, counting on making up any slack with private parties.

We had only one thorn in our side: Manitas de Plata, the famous guitarist. At that time, he was not yet well known, but was a fabulous talent trying his hand busking in the St. Tropez restaurant scene. It seemed he was always playing at the same club we were. As soon as we heard he would be sharing the bill, we knew our take would be reduced.

Manitas de Plata was a total gypsy. He had a wife and ten or eleven children, all of whom came with him when he played. They'd eat big slices of bread and drink wine right from their mother's glass. Manitas would strum his flamenco guitar and his kids would all be singing "Ai-ai-ai-ai!" They were like miniature flamenco dancers with tight little costumes. They'd click their heels and spin with their arms above their heads, snapping their fingers like castanets.

Customers tossed in a lot of money when his hat was passed because the children were all so cute. People figured he needed a real income with all those mouths to feed. Of course, he was also an outstanding musician. We seemed more self-sufficient, without children, so our take would usually be less than his.

We had the use of several luxurious cars during the summer. My friend David Hamilton, who owned houses in Ramatuelle and London, lent us his Astin Martin while he returned to England. Instead of storing it in Nice, he just gave it to us for a while.

A Canadian recording executive lent us his Jaguar XKE for two weeks. This was a very flashy car, an absolute head-turner. One evening during the time we were using this car, Ruth and I put on an exceptional show at Chez Ferdinand. We had an adequate take, but nothing like the usual, considering the size of the crowd. It seemed to us that the customers that night were particularly snotty. We happened to be leaving at the same time as a table of wealthy Parisians, and they saw us hop into the XKE outside the restaurant.

"Oh, the buskers drive an XKE!"

This didn't put anything in our pockets, but it was sweet revenge nonetheless.

The Jag and Astin Martin loved the open roads, but when we drove into Ramatuelle, with its tiny zig-zagging streets, the cars often just died. We'd laugh, get out, and give a quick push-start.

The Canadian recording exec lent us the XKE because he wanted to entice us into flying to Canada to talk with his home office about signing a recording contract. We thought about it seriously, but Canada seemed such a long way away, and the St. Tropez season was in full spin. We kept putting it off and putting it off.

For the time being, our singing, which by that time had become polished and professional, was edging out our interests in painting and sculpture. We spent most of the day either performing or practicing. It was fun, make no mistake. We both loved music, and it was providing us with a healthy bank balance and instantaneous gratification.

When people liked our performances, they threw bills into the hat and applauded. (When someone likes a painting, they go home and think about it for a year or so.)

Neither of us were the types to let grass grow under our feet. We sensed an opportunity. Hell, musicians with far less to offer had made it big.

We had a pleasant nodding acquaintance with the lovely Ms. Bardot. We played at quite a few of her soirees, and she always was gracious and friendly to us. About his time, she became engaged to one of St. Tropez's leading personalities, Gunther Sachs, an enormously wealthy playboy. He enjoyed the reputation of being the ultimate debonaire jet-setter. He could be seen almost any evening in one of the many trendy clubs with a bevy of beautiful women preening for his delight. Gunter, in his own right, was where things were happening. Brigette was an incandescent star. Gunter and Brigette together? You can imagine. They cornered the market.

Newspapers and magazines from St. Tropez to London spotlighted this fairytale romance. The local Chamber of Commerce was ecstatic. Even we had to admit that it was dazzling stuff. Especially since the couple of the moment recognized us on sight and went out of their way to be cordial.

One evening, after an unusually successful performance at Chez Fernand, we were passed a note asking us to join a table for drinks. This was hardly out of the ordinary, so we agreed. We were used to that sort of thing by now. It was all part of the gig. A jovial, somewhat rotund gentleman, brimming with good nature and wine, stood and introduced himself and his wife with a nearly imperceptible but definite click of the heels. "Hans and Gretel Wiener, from Munich," he said.

"May I also have the pleasure," he added, "of presenting Herr Deiter Gelt, of Hamburg." With that introduction, I heard a resounding heel click.

Compliments gushed like a fractured water main. Our guests poured drinks, and the evening rolled along, happy as a summer hayride.

After the second or third round, Hans and Herr Gelt leaned forward for a confidential chat with me. Gretel had maneuvered Ruth into a discussion about the current trends in ladies' summer apparel.

"We are finding much interest in you and your partner in ze zinging," Hans said. He pulled his chair a little closer and poured more cognac. "Herr Gelt is with Polydor Records. Zey are ze largest record company in Ze Germany. He is wanting that we should see if we can do somezing for you." His smile lighted the restaraunt. Herr Gelt nodded and downed his drink.

Oh! Talk to me, I thought. *Talk to me!*

In the course of the conversation, I learned that Gunther Sachs had mentioned Ruth and me to Fritz Von Opel (the same Opel whose name was on half the cars in Europe.) Herr Opel had in turn mentioned us to Herr Gelt's boss, who had then mentioned us to Herr Gelt, who happened to be visiting Herr Weiner in St. Tropez.

I managed to pry Ruth away from Gretel long enough to fill her in. We acknowledged that this was indeed something worthy of serious consideration. We agreed to lunch the following day at Hans's rented villa for further discussion. The evening ended with hand kissing, hand shaking, slaps on the shoulder, encouragement, reassurances, felicitations, and more heel clicking.

Ruth and I were dizzy. We drove down to Senequiers on the Port for a late coffee and reflected on the evening's turn of events.

We felt, once again, on a rollercoaster. One may want to get off, but while it's moving that can be very difficult. For the moment, we decided to savor the thrill. We had been offered a contract with the largest recording company in Europe. Overnight our status had leapt from street musicians to professional recording artists. We were completly seduced by the prospects.

We had other reasons to take the offer seriously. The season was coming to an end. Our three mainstay restaurants were showing the first signs of slowing. We were already noticing decreased tips, and the boat parties and private gigs were becoming fewer.

Our season of semi-fame was closing. Everything had happened so quickly that we hadn't made plans. We truly had been living the moment. Perhaps fate was giving us a nudge, we thought.

You must realize that we knew absolutely nothing about the music business — or indeed about any business. We were artists on a lark. We sang, were paid, and rushed back to our flat, where we locked the money in a big box. That was the extent of our business acumen. We ate well, swam, sunbathed, played guitars, and painted whenever we could. In every respect we enjoyed a carefree existence, with no thought of anything past the next evening.

The idea of turning pro by signing a recording contract was frightening. But it also stroked our egos. It gave us confidence. "See, someone who knows about these things thinks we're good!"

It was September, month of languid days. The sun was still warm, but weakening. The balmy atmosphere of St. Tropez, with its thinning crowds and cooler evening air, was one to drink and savor. But time and tide rushed us. We felt obliged to face reality. We had precious little money saved, and even a slight success in the recording business, we felt, could buy us a period of freedom. Many serious discussions between Ruth and myself ended with one overriding conclusion: if we could put aside a little money singing, we might be able to carve out some time to do nothing but paint.

We decided to charge ahead. Herr Gelt phoned his office, and several days later a big cheese from Hamburg arrived. He was a round, jovial, middle-aged man who liked mainstream jazz, schnapps, and sausage.

He watched us perform at one of our favorite spots. That evening we outdid ourselves. The crowd even gave us a standing ovation. The producer was in our hip pocket. He couldn't find enough superlatives. He assured us that, if we signed with his company, we could count on success

The next morning, he phoned headquarters. Within a week, representatives from the recording company in Hamburg, the publishing house in Stuttgart, and the management company in Munich all flew down. We met with them at Hans's rented house. Amid reassurances, pats on the back, and quickly emptying bottles of wine, we signed a ten-year recording, publishing, and personal management contract.

I felt a twinge of apprehension. The documents were completely in German, and we had no legal counsel. My fears evaporated as more wine flowed. "Everything will be fine!" "A great opportunity!" "New stars in the firmament of the music world." *Ausgezeichnet! Jawohl!!*

In this one moment, we signed away our musical careers to a group of German businessmen. We received zero up-front monies and no compensation whatsoever.

What on earth were we doing? Why would two musicians who sang mostly American folk songs sign a contract in German, with Germans? And why would they be so interested in us? I was a painter and Ruth a sculptor. Our sole means of income had been singing in the streets surrounded by the glorified carnival life of St. Tropez. Anyone with half a mind would have known this was not the basis for a successful career.

To our credit, occasionally we shared a lingering doubt that perhaps we had signed up with the wrong lot. What could Germans know of American folk music? But adventure lay ahead of us. We had the energy of youth and the spirit of the indefatigable.

The St. Tropez season ended. Beaches emptied. The harbor filled with yachts put up for the winter. Restaurants became quiet. The sun grew weaker, and the locals resumed the rituals of provincial life. They reclaimed their "Boule" patch, free of the clutter of tourists. It was easier to do the day's shopping. Bread was fresher, wine easier to find, and sleep undisturbed by late parties.

It was time for us to leave, time for the next part of our story. We would return to London and await the call from our German producers.

24

Biding Time in London

During our trip from St. Tropez to London, the relation ship between Ruth and me changed from singing partners to lovers.

All very well and good, but it complicated an already confusing situation. The last thing Ruth and I should have done was become involved emotionally. We were asking for trouble. Artists at heart, we were swimming out of our element after signing the recording contract. Perhaps we tried to make something solid out of our lives by clinging to each other.

Love is never very happy in that position. We both chose to ignore the obvious, and accommodated the double status of lovers/singing partners as casually and with as little attention as possible.

We arrived in London during early October. Summer had slipped away, along with cricket matches at Lords, boating on the Serpentine and walks on Hampstead Heath.

The year was 1967. Life in London was one long dance. Pop groups sprung up like weeds. New fashions caught hold overnight. It was the era of the miniskirt, which allowed women to parade in public wearing little more than a brief sarong. Since Ruth had a pair of legs nothing short of spectacular, the new fashion was right up her alley.

We stayed with friends while waiting instructions from the

German recording company. The accommodations were cramped, and we felt our presence very much of an imposition. Every day we rushed to the door to greet the mail. It became a ritual. As days passed, Ruth and I noticed that our hosts, Richard and Penelope, became almost as eager to open the mail as we.

Richard, a friend from university days, was a writer who had enjoyed considerable success with a TV series six years previously. Having produced nothing since then, he seemed quite content to bask in the short glory and diminishing royalties of the past.

We watched his daily preparations for writing. They were unvarying and always ended with the same results: zero production. Going through a pack of cigarettes and half a fifth of gin while sitting at the typewriter waiting for his muse to arrive seemed to slow his typing speed.

However, he had considerable experience in the world of show biz and explained some of the intricacies of contracts and royalties. He was concerned that our negotiations had been shaky, to say the least.

A few of his professional friends came round for drinks one day. They agreed that we had signed an unusually long contract. Ten years was unheard of, they said. Maybe five, or more commonly two or three, with renegotiation at that point to allow increased benefits should success arrive. They also assured us that it was customary for publishers to provide a guarantee, such as an advance of cash or a monthly stipend. We certainly had not been provided with any such luxuries. The theory behind such a guarantee of funds is that artists need at least a semblance of security to produce their best work. After all, how creative and energetic can someone be when scrounging the next meal?

Hindsight is always 20/20. There was not much to do about the situation, unless we simply rejected the whole idea and went on to something else. We had no work in London, so simply walking away from the contract would set us back to square one. Not a very exciting prospect.

25

Mrs. Manicotte

After a week, we still had not heard from our German connection. Relations with Richard and Penelope became too strained, so Ruth and I began looking for our own temporary lodgings.

I had learned that one must be particularly careful when renting a London flat in October. All too often, premises that appear quite splendid in autumn become untenantable in the freezing winds of November.

We were introduced to an elderly lady with a top-floor flat for rent in her house on Ravenna Road, just off Putney High Street. Hers was a pleasant building of late Victorian vintage, with a small garden and a gate that had seen better days.

Come to think of it, the entire house had seen better days, although it showed great charm and was convenient. Flats at that time were hard to come by. Since we did not know how long we would have to stay in London, we were assured by friends that we should snap it up.

We were met at the front door by the owner, Mrs. Manicotte. She was a frail, elderly lady with bluish grey hair, twinkling eyes, and a warm smile. Her voice and manner were quietly refined. In another era she would have been quite at home in a baronial manor.

"You must be the young couple looking for a room. I was told to expect you. Do come in."

She showed us into the hallway. It was dark and rather musty, with the inevitable coat stand and a withered aspidistra in a brass pot.

"I've got the kettle on. Will you take some tea?"

We were ushered into her sitting room at the rear of the ground floor.

Now that was a room which had been lived in. It had not an inch of wall space without a photograph or piece of memorabilia. The entire room was so tightly cramped there was hardly space to move. We found a couple of chairs and dutifully sipped the offered tea, each taking a digestive biscuit from a coronation tin.

We explained our situation, and she seemed perfectly content to take us on a week-by-week basis. "I'll enjoy you while you're with me," she said. "When you have to go, that will be that."

Although our flat on the third floor was without bath, toilet, or running water for the kitchen, we made it quite homey. An elaborate pulley system enabled us to raise large buckets of water without having to run up and down. It reminded us, in ways, of our rustic cabenon in Ramatuelle.

Mrs. Manicotte was a jolly lady with a dazzling history. We got to know her quite well during the next several weeks. She had toured the world as a dancer, performing before Russian royalty, the maharajas of India, and theatre audiences in the United States. She had a soft spot for New York, winking and calling it "a thoroughly wicked city."

What tales Mrs. Manicotte had to tell. It seemed unfitting that her glorious life should end in a rundown house in the arse end of Putney.

It didn't bother her a whit.

"As a dancer one has a very short career. You have to make the most of it while the body is cooperative. When it's over, it's over!"

We helped with shopping and the all-important task of replenishing her sherry supply. Aside from that, she was completely self-sufficient, content to live out her solitary existence.

When still a young woman, she had lived with one of the famous French Impressionists, whom she steadfastly refused to name. One day, in great confidence, she took from beneath her bed a stack of unframed canvasses.

I swear they were original Pissarros.

Can you imagine the value of those today? We tried to persuade her to take them for appraisal, or at least have them framed for safekeeping. She assured us that she would consider neither.

Such exquisite beauty. The paintings were, essentialy, a museum wall full of genius crammed beneath a bed amidst old socks and frayed tissues.

When we were shown those paintings, Ruth commented that when first arriving in London she had stayed at a house with two original Chagalls hung casually on the stairway wall. They had been given to the landlady decades before when she had been a student of the master.

Perhaps Ruth's landlady, as Mrs. Manicotte, preferred to keep such intimate memories close at hand and private, away from the clutching eyes of the unsympathetic.

26
Blurred Edges

October turned to November, and still we were rushing to the mail each morning. Our funds were low, and we were thinking of approaching some of the local clubs to pick up a few extra shillings. It would have had to be on a short-term basis. That's not to the liking of most club owners.

We spent our time sketching and painting. Our third-floor flat was warm and comfortable. We turned it into a studio, with easels by the window and canvas flopped willy-nilly.

This respite from singing was gratifying. If only we had a source of income, we thought. Our situation was uncertain to the extreme, but we made the best of it.

One particularly frigid afternoon, we noticed that our rooms had suddenly gone cold. The gas fire had gone out.

I threw on a sweater and rushed downstairs to speak with Mrs. Manicotte. She was in her room, swathed in a large blanket, sipping her sherry.

"We seem to have lost our heat," I said.

The house had become several degrees colder just in the time it had taken me to get downstairs.

"Did you pay the gas bill last week?" I asked. "Remember, I offered to take it down for you?"

"Oh, dear. I wonder. Do you know, I can't remember whether I did or not. I tend to lose track of these things." She pulled her blanket a little closer and took another sip of sherry.

"Mrs. Manicotte, I'm going straight down to the gas company and pay the bill out of my own pocket. The pipes will freeze."

She was a dear, but this was ridiculous.

"Perhaps that would be a good idea, but don't pay all of it. Just enough so they come by and turn it on again. Spring's coming. Then we can see to all the bills and such."

November, and spring was coming?

She fumbled in her purse and pulled out a five-pound note. "Since you're going, perhaps you could stop by and get another bottle of sherry?"

As you can tell, we were getting to be quite good friends. I decided to tell it to her straight.

"Don't you think it would be a lot wiser to pay the damned gas bill? I mean, first things first!"

She smiled a knowing smile.

"Dear, when you reach my age you'll find it's preferable to put a little blur on the edges." She handed me the note. "Don't forget the sherry there's a dear."

We managed to get the gas turned on the next day. By some miracle the pipes didn't burst and no one froze.

Maybe she had a point.

27
Gladys The Tiger Lady

We had been in London almost a month when we decided we had to make a move. We were nearly out of money, and the daily rites of waiting for the mail was driving us to the edge.

We thought that instead of approaching clubs directly, we might try contacting an agent, who could set us up with short-term engagements around the city. I made a few calls, and by the next morning we had an offer for a one-week gig in northern England. I thought it rather unusual that the agent hadn't even found it necessary to see us perform. "You sound like a nice chap," he said, "and folk music really is the thing now. Aren't those Beatles doing well?"

The booking turned out to be at The Carlton, a nightclub in my home town of Chesterfield! We would also be required to do an early show each day at a working men's club in a neighboring town.

There wasn't much to debate. We needed an infusion of cash, and I looked forward to going home. It would be fun to return to the scene of my youth as a full-fledged star.

So it came about that on a damp foggy morning, with London engulfed in a classic Pea Souper, we piled our guitars and suitcases into our tiny car and set out to bring joy and music to the great northern populace.

The enveloping fog obscured everything in a thick odious blanket of soot and smoke. Traffic was sluggish, and we continually missed turns and road signs. The fog lifted around Newark, and we arrived at my mother's house in time for afternoon tea and scones.

Mother wasn't thrilled at the prospect of my singing in the local nightclub. As far as she was concerned, The Carlton was nothing more than a den of vice populated by the scum of the earth. How a son of hers could end up in such a place was beyond her comprehension. After all, I had a college education. Why wasn't I using it? When was I ever going to amount to something? And exposing this sweet young American girl to such a thing! Disgraceful. But of course no one ever listened to her. Have another scone, dear, you look thin.

Staying at Mother's perhaps wasn't the best idea, but it saved us the cost of a bed and breakfast.

Like many northern clubs, The Carlton was a masterpiece of atmosphere. Plastic vines wrapping around artificial columns. Dimly lit tables with candles flickering in red plastic pots. A stage with a couple of cheap spotlights. The fragrance of stale beer and spilt wine. And mirrors everywhere. What people like most, after all, is looking at themselves.

We arrived mid-afternoon to scout the place. A jovial man greeted us. He offered a drink and showed us the facilities.

"First show's at ten. It starts to fill up when the pubs let out. Second show at twelve."

He swaggered to the stage. Ruth and I examined the speakers and microphone, trying to make some sense out of the archaic sound system.

"Don't worry, kids. They'll be legless by the second set. Keep it loud and happy and you'll be fine!"

He smoothed his slicked-back hair and scratched his groin. Not knowing what more to say, he returned to the bar to take up where he had left off with his girlfriend, a middle-aged blonde with inches of makeup and yards of cleavage.

We did a sound check. Everything seemed to work, but we decided that we were entirely in fate's hands.

Our early show each evening was to be at The Worksop

Working Man's Club, an enormous barn of a building on the grounds of the local colliery. The colliery had established the club to provide recreation and diversion for the miners, who spent ten hours every day digging coal half a mile below ground.

At the end of their shifts, the miners were brought to the surface. After a shower and a quick meal they wandered over to the Workingmens Club to down pints of warm bitter and anesthetize themselves until their next shifts below ground.

We arrived at the club late in the afternoon and wandered into the main hall, which was already packed with drinkers. You could smell the spilt day-old booze on the floor. The air was stifling with cigarette smoke. On stage at the far end of the hall, an extremely overweight and jovial man played renditions of oldies on a giant Hammond organ. When he caught sight of us, he went into a blazing crescendo, closed the lid, and took a bow.

A few of the drinkers applauded, but believe me it was very, very light. People were not there for the entertainment.

The musician waddled over to us.

"'Ello. The singers, right? I'm Chubby."

Enormous would have been a more appropriate name. At least he was friendly.

"I sort of emcee here. Changin' room's out back. Not fancy mind, but it serves. You'll be goin' on at eight."

The changing room was no more than a small storage closet full of empty beer crates and boxes of potato crisps. Ruth and I changed into our performing clothes and sat back. Entertainers, like soldiers, spend a lot of time waiting.

Meanwhile, goodtime Chubby lashed the Hammond into melodies that were, at best, crucifixions of popular favorites. As the volume of the crowd increased, so did the volume of the music. This was not going to be pretty.

There was a knock on the door. A middle-aged lady entered.

"Is this the changing room?" she asked in a meek, little-girl voice.

We quickly learned that she was to precede us on stage. We hadn't known there would be an act before us, but somehow this miscommunication wasn't surprising. To let her dress, we edged our way out into the main hall, where the bacchanal was in full swing. The amount of beer and whiskey going down made the Oktoberfest in Munich seem like a ladies' tea at Claridges.

Chubby ground to the end of a spirited rendition of "Strangers in the Night," milking the giant organ for every watt it had. The final crescendo sounded as though he sat on half the keys simultaneously.

This was again followed by light applause, and Chubby stepped to the microphone. He slimed the audience with a massive smile, oozing good humor and suave confidence. He tapped the microphone with several quick jabs. These reverberated through the hall like bazooka fire and actually attracted some attention from the crowd.

Launching into patter swift as a machine gun, Chubby's foghorn voice riveted those sober enough to keep their heads erect.

"Ladies and gentlemen, we've got a grand show for you this evenin'. You're goin' to love it."

It was almost threatening. A challenge.

"We've spared no expense, and as always here at the club, we take great pride in presentin' only the best in entertainment. Later you'll be treated to a wonderful new act all the way from London, fresh from a triumphant tour of the continent."

He waved his arms, for no reason I could determine.

"But right now, it's time to get the show started! Here's a local lass destined for stardom and the silver screen. I want you all to give a real Worksop welcome to our first turn on the bill. Here's . . . GLADYS THE TIGER LADY!"

With a display of athletic ability incredible for a man his size, Chubby leapt onto the organ stool and began pounding out a musical introduction. If there had been house lights, they would have dimmed. But there were none and they didn't.

Out pranced the lady we had met in the changing room.

Poor thing, she had seen better days. She had tits out to tomorrow, but the rest of her body sagged in all the wrong places. Clad in a scanty tiger costume and wearing a papier-mache tiger mask with terminal mange, she tried to gyrate her way across stage in her high heels. Chubby belted away at the Hammond, giving musical enhancement to this would-be striptease.

Gladys the Tiger Lady fumbled with a piece of her costume and tossed it aside seductively. As she did, a heel caught and she nearly tripped. Her act could have been a classic piece of comedy. Unfortunately, the audience took it seriously.

No wonder. This was the closest thing to a sexual encounter most of them would have for the remainder of their lives. Their attention was rapt. Glasses continued to be emptied and refilled, but all eyes were on Gladys as she swayed and stripped in her spastic dance routine.

Finally, down to her bra and panties, she made a valiant effort to move to the side curtains. Just before exiting, she gave a little flourish of the bum.

Too bad.

She tripped again and got tangled in some loose wiring, falling with a sickening thud to the floor. In a final vortex of limbs, masks, and panties, she managed to crawl off stage.

The crowd went wild. It had been the greatest act they had ever seen.

They stood. They screamed. They whistled. They wanted more.

Chubby raised his arms for quiet, assuring everyone that if Gladys's injuries weren't too serious, she would be back later.

The crowd didn't buy it. They kept shouting, chanting for an encore.

"And now," the undauntable Chubby announced, "for a change of pace let's give a warm round of applause for two lovely song birds. Ladies and gentlemen — Ruth and Kerry!"

We were on.

There was no way out.

We hopped up on stage and died.

The miners took one look at us and turned back to their beer. After Gladys, who at least offered the possibility of baring some boob, we could supply them absolutely nothing of interest. They knew it at a glance.

We tried a little humorous patter. No response.

We launched into a song. Nothing. The decibel level of conversation and clinking glasses increased. The miners ordered more beer. They ordered more whiskey. "Ay up, John, cum an 'ave a chair! 'Ow are ya?" They completely forgot about us.

After twenty minutes giving it our all, we'd had enough. We couldn't hear ourselves sing. We couldn't even harmonize. At times, we weren't even sure we were singing the same song. I caught Ruth's eye and with a nod we agreed to abbreviate the set. Just as we were beginning what was to be the last number, Chubby joined in. He had no idea what song we were singing, but that didn't stop him. Really, to be honest, what did it matter?

With his ravishing smile and complete lack of musical ability, he pounded away on his trusty Hammond until our voices were lost in a cacophony reminiscent of the Blitzkrieg.

The applause was sparse. Hardly surprising, since most of the audience had long forgotten we were on stage.

With a rather dubious sense of occasion, Chubby tried to call us back for an encore. Ruth fixed him with a withering stare. Chubby was crestfallen. For him, this was a perfectly normal evening.

"Well, right then. I'll have to bring Gladys back. Pity though. The crowd was just warming up."

O to be blessed with such cheerful insensibility.

We left for the Carlton Club, carrying the sobering thought that this was to be our lot every night for a week.

28
The Carlton Club

When we arrived at The Carlton, most tables were still empty. A few people sat deep in their drinking. The room was a somber sight that did not bode well.

I had spent most of the afternoon persuading Mother to come. This was very much against her principles and would be a first for her. I might as well have asked her to visit Hades for the evening. It was a disgrace and no mistake. But since I was her only son and still worthy of her support, she agreed.

When Ruth and I arrived, Mother was sitting with Mrs. Rhodes, her next door neighbor. Mother felt a little better knowing that she would die in the company of a friend. They took a seat in a particularly dark corner. Still in their overcoats, they clutched their handbags as if ready to flee at the first sign of trouble.

We joined them for a drink and did our best to lighten the mood. Mother was determined that this was going to be living hell — and that was that. Ruth and I went backstage to ready ourselves.

The manager, whom we had met earlier that afternoon, came back to wish us good luck.

"Don't worry, the first house is always a bit light. The pubs don't close till eleven."

He gave us a quick smile and a pat on the back. As all seasoned club managers know, it's not a good idea to identify too closely with those about to do battle.

Halfway through our second number, three of my guitar strings broke simultaneously. That must be one for Guiness. I've had one string go on me a few times. That's manageable. You just fake chords, working around the broken string. But three? It was impossible to produce any sort of harmonious sound. All I could do was smile and pretend nothing was wrong. Ruth somehow managed to carry us through the first set.

No one really noticed or cared. As the manager had tactfully pointed out, it was a thin house.

The strings took nearly an hour to change. They seemed to have a life of their own.

The second set wasn't much better. I forgot the words to a couple of songs and hit some off chords. But we survived. The first evening's performance was behind us.

The manager came backstage. He was concerned, his brow furrowed. "This folk stuff is all very nice," he said, "but it's not quite 'on' for a nightclub, is it?" Did we have a few popular numbers that the folks could sing along with on following evenings? Perhaps "Michael Row Your Boat Ashore"? "Yellow Ribbon"? "Country Roads"? Something along that line?

It was obvious that we weren't what he had hoped for. For him, the act on stage was completely secondary to the consumption of alcohol at the tables and bar. Who could blame him? Consumption was where profits lay. Performers could do whatever they wanted, as long as they did not interrupt the consumption of booze.

Happy people were drinking people. Quiet people needed to be rousted out of their silence and cajoled into feeling that they were having the time of their lives. The performers were expected to provide the right backdrop. The louder the better. Our obscure and relatively introspective renderings were not at all what was needed.

We told him that we fully understood but were at a loss. We had a specific set of songs that we had carefully chosen and rehearsed, and we were stuck with those for the moment. We assured him that we would try to come up with a few numbers to fit his needs, but that was the best we could promise.

"See what you can do, will you? We need summat they know. Summat to get 'em up. It's all down to 'avin a good time like."

Even my mother was unexcited. She didn't say much on the way home, but I'm sure she wondered about my sanity. I was wondering about it myself.

Next morning I awoke with acute laryngitis. My voice had almost completely deserted me. Thoroughly depressed, I dragged myself off to the local doctor. He told me there wasn't a thing he could do to help my voice return to full strength in time for the evening's vocal marathon.

I wandered into a nearby pub to drown my sorrows. The barmaid was a crusty old dame I remembered from my misspent youth. Over a glass I told her my predicament.

"Ee lad, don't worry. We'll fix you right up. Ah used to be on the 'alls meself when Ah was a lass. Ther' weren't no mikes in them days. We 'ad to belt it out as best we could. Ah'll make thee a drink that'll get thee through."

She returned with a glass of dark brown liquid.

"Sip it slow like, let it run down thee throat. Finish a coupla them an ya'll be right as rain."

It was a warmed mixture of port wine, honey, and lemon juice. Looked evil but didn't taste half bad. I downed the glass, then a second. Within half an hour, my voice was inching back.

Through the afternoon I had five or six more glasses of the brew. By evening, I was almost able to speak in full voice. By the time we went on, I was able to sustain a note. Truthfully, I was to the point at which, ably medicated, I didn't care what I sounded like.

We sailed through the sets at the Worksop and The Carlton oblivious of the reception. We didn't care if we could or could not be heard. The night was an exercise in survival. We kept telling ourselves that there was a valid reason for this madness. We were in the middle of a grand design, a bigger picture.

I still haven't figured out what that might have been.

29

To the Altar

Six nights later, we crawled back to London. Mrs. Manicotte, sitting in her robe and blanket, sipping a sherry, welcomed us merrily. We tossed ourselves on the bed and fell asleep in our clothes.

Next morning, I recall, was cold and bright. We took stock of our situation, feeling perhaps that we would never hear from our German producers. We sent them off a telegram, politely reminding them of our existence, and made plans for a winter in London in case they remained elusive.

We debated chucking the whole thing and returning to our art. But we were broke, and tired of being so. We had come this far in music, and knew that by this time our singing was much better than the average folk duo's. We were sure that, given the right circumstances, we could produce an album of original and innovative music.

Ruth's voice and persona were certainly worthy of recognition and development. For my part, I had an able enough voice, some flair for songwriting, and a pleasing stage personality. This combination gave us a reasonable shot. Taking our careers in hand, we began going from agent to agent, trying to find someone who would recognise our talents and provide exposure.

Time drifted. A few more weeks went by, and we seemed no further along than when we had returned from St. Tropez.

During one of our many flirtations with prospective promoters, we were persuaded that it would be a good move to enhance our image of "The Romantic Singing Duo." We were encouraged to think seriously about getting married — as a career move. The promoter pointed out that, since we were living together and quite obviously madly in love anyway, as young people often are, such a step would be entirely appropriate.

I think we allowed ourselves to buy into this idea more out of frustration than from any deep romantic attachment. We figured that it was perhaps a good idea to confirm the myth — if it helped us move toward the success that we felt we so richly deserved.

Ruth and I had a lot in common and certainly liked and respected each other. As we were to discover, this is substantially different from being committed to a lifetime relationship.

We talked ourselves into the idea and began preparations for the show biz marriage of the century. This was music to the promoter's ears. He assured us that the wedding would be the final ingredient, virtually guaranteeing our success.

We prepared for the big day in much the same way that we did for a concert. For us, there seemed little difference. It was another gig that would be good or bad depending on the reception.

A cold, bleak December day dawned, and we were presented like lambs to the slaughter at the Kensington Registers Office. We were pronounced Man and Wife with all the pizzazz and fanfare of a damp firecracker.

There was no press.

No photographers clambering for candid shots of the soon-to-be-famous couple.

No speeches.

Nothing to mark the event as anything more than another nondescript nuptial ceremony. It would soon be forgotten, along with all the others that would take place that week.

Ruth and I both knew that we had cast a substantial die. Neither of us took the institution of marriage lightly. We had entered uncharted waters. This was serious stuff.

The days that followed were strained. The promotor turned out to be no more reliable or productive than the others we had encountered. His prospective bookings for us were a joke, hardly better than our run at The Carlton. We saw right through them and passed on the opportunity.

Ruth was overwrought. She was so on edge that a doctor prescribed mild tranquilizers. This calmed things down a bit, but we were both in something of a tailspin.

Just when it seemed things could get no worse, we received a telegram from our publishers, inviting us to Munich. Winter had set in hard, and London seemed a series of closed doors. Ruth and I decided that the best thing to do was make the trip and see what came of it. If things went as well as promised, we could face the contractual difficulties after gaining the leverage of becoming a "hot property." Or, at least, we could record an album, beg for an advance, then hop a plane to somewhere warm and set up easels in the sun.

30
Schnapps and Fizzle

We arrived at Munich airport with all the pomp and circumstance of a defrocked minister. No fanfare, no limousine, no indication that we were stars in the making. The producer's wife, Gretel, wearing thick rhinestone glasses and flamboyant stretch pants, was the only person waiting for us. She whisked us off at high speed in a bland little car to a small hotel in Grunwald, a suburb of Munich.

We had the oddest feeling that we were being hidden!

If anything, it was even colder in Germany than in England. As we got out of the car, we bundled up against the wind, which seemed to be attacking from all directions at the same time.

Grunwald was one of the few Munich suburbs that had survived the obliterative bombing during the closing days of World War Two. It had an air of antiquity. Historic buildings lined the streets. One felt that this region had played an important, long-standing role in European history. Notable was the pristine neatness permeating everything: immaculate roads, newly painted fences, carefully manicured lawns and gardens. It seemed that even the patches of snow remaining from the last storm had been freshly washed and polished.

Gretel bade farewell and vanished, leaving us on our own. We settled into the hotel and began acclimating to Germany.

During the long occupation of the Allied forces after the war, many Germans had learned to speak English. This allowed them at least to communicate with two would-be English rock stars holed up in an out-of-the way German hotel room.

Next day Hans gave us a hasty lunch at his home. He threw in a lightning tour of his neighborhood, then excused himself, saying he was late for an appointment with his publisher.

Ruth and I spent the next several days playing tourist, trying to tap into the German lifestyle. We put on brave faces for each other, pretending to be at ease, like big shots knowing exactly what we were doing and where we were going.

Secretly, we were worried to death thinking about the impending meeting with the company's recording executives. Everyone who was anyone in the company would be there, Hans had informed us.

At last our nervousness got the better of us. We sat down to examine the pros and cons of our situation. The main con was that we had nearly run out of money. We were living on savings from St. Tropez and the laughable earnings from the Carlton gig. The costs of our flight to Munich and our hotel stay were being met by the recording company, but we were paying for our own meals.

We discussed all this and decided that it did not seem quite right. Yet here we were, in the middle of it, so what could we do? We had tried to broach the subject earlier with Hans, but didn't want to push too hard because we felt it a delicate subject.

Of course, there's nothing delicate about spending one's own money on someone else's venture. It was sheer stupidity on our part. As naive artists/folk singers, we hadn't yet grasped that. We were still locked into an attitude of gratitude to our would-be benefactors, who to that point had shown us nothing.

Our discussion went round and round. Inevitably, we came full circle to our original feelings: that we were entirely in their hands. We decided that the best course was to move forward and see what happened.

Next afternoon we arrived at the producer's home in our best outfits, complete with guitars and dry mouths. This was

the big day. When we were shown into the lounge, the chief
recording executive and his three publishers, along with Hans
and his wife, were already in a jovial Bavarian haze of schnapps
and beer. The ensuing introductions were pleasant, but tense.
Everyone spoke such heavily accented English that it was difficult to take the situation seriously. The scene was like a film
caricature of drunken Germans trying to speak English.

After many perfunctory niceties, they asked us to perform
a few songs. We sang with as much gusto and verve as the
situation allowed, rattling through "Wabash Cannonball,"
"Homeward Bound," and a couple of Dylan numbers.

Our small but select audience stood and applauded. We
had passed! There were felicitations, congratulations, and compliments. Schnapps and beer all around, then all around again.
Then down to the local restaurant for venison and more
schnapps, followed by coffee and cognac.

Ruth and I were in high spirits. Everything was going won-
derfully. All our fears, it seemed, had been unfounded. These
were delightful, well-meaning people.

We returned to Hans's home, and the schnapps continued
to flow. We exchanged a few jokes. We told stories of our
busking days in St. Tropez and about our fortunate meeting
with Hans and his wife. There were good spirits and warm
feelings all around. The evening relaxed into a convivial, almost festive affair.

The chief recording executive rose from his chair with some
difficulty, trying to work his way through the schnapps.

"Vell, Kerry and Root, I zink ze zongs are ver gut. Ze sing-
ing — ver gut — excellent. But, you know, here in Germany ve
Germans like to hear ze zongs, *auf Deutch*. Or, as you say, in ze
German.

"Zere is ze great potential 'ere. Ze big starz are 'ere. Ve
mussen making sure zat we are choosink ver gut zongs for zer
first album. I sink you go back to England und learn four songs
auf Deutch, zen we talk again. *Jawohl.*"

He laughed a Bavarian belly laugh and downed another
schnapps.

Ruth and I exchanged a furtive glance. We both knew exactly what the other was thinking. Our worst fears had come
alive.

There was a very long pause. Then the recording people resumed conversation in German, leaving Ruth and me to sit in a state of stunned silence. What could we do? How on earth were we to learn four German songs? And how were we supposed to return to England?

"Excuse me," I spoke up. "It's a bit difficult for us. We have very little money left from this trip. And we have no place to return to in England. We . . . er . . . thought we would be taken care of, since we signed your contract."

The chief executive turned a benign face toward us. He smiled, then laughed. It was the kind of laughter that follows an amusing story. Not exactly a belly laugh, but a really good solid laugh. As though waiting for their cue, the others started to laugh, too.

After a minute or two, the chief executive gathered his composure.

"Oh, Kerry, my friend. Ve are not able to pay you ze wage at ze moment. Ve do not know ou ze album vill zell. It is zer expensive to make ze albums. Oh, no. You must make ze German zongs. Ve are ere in Germany, no? Yes? Zen, vy zing ze zongs in Englitch?"

He lifted his glass and dove into a fresh schnapps.

At that point I was completely deflated. My wind was gone, my stomach in knots. The producer motioned the chief aside. For several minutes, they huddled in the corner, whispering quietly and glancing occasionally in our direction. Coming to some sort of agreement, they returned to the group, all smiles.

"Herr Weiner has a great und sehr generous idea. He and his gut wife will find akomodation and feed for ze two for one mons. Und you will learn six German zongs, yes? Ve vill begin ze rekordink in six weeks."

Everyone agreed that this was such a profound act of generosity that we should kneel and kiss the feet of Herr Hans. The group gave him hearty congratulations, and the party dissolved amidst handshakes and backslaps, and one more schnapps for the road.

As everyone else went into the entranceway to leave, Ruth and I sat in the quiet of the lounge. I could tell she was close to tears. I could hardly blame her. I wasn't that far away myself.

Hans and Gretel, having sent the recording executives on their schnapps-accelerated way, returned after a few minutes. "Well, very gut," said Hans. "Tomorrow ve vill find some rooms for you and begin ze work. My wife has kindly agreed to teach you ze German. She vill translate ze words, zen all vill be good. Now ve say *guten nacht* please to call ze taxi." We returned to the hotel in a taxi. It was probably the most humiliating night of my life. Somehow, Ruth and I managed to console each other. Desolation gave way to resignation, but the embarrassment and disappointment remained. They had treaded us shabbily, no doubt about it. We had been very cleverly had. Our friends in London had been right. Contracts are only as good as the spirit that goes with them (and the money sitting on the table).

After a fitful sleep, the telephone awakened us. Hans had located accommodations. "You would please to pack and ready to move in one half hour. *Jawohl?*"

We taxied to an address on a completely forgettable street in a nameless Munich suburb. We waited on the curb until Hans arrived, then followed him up the front steps.

Looking up at the house we were to live in, it seemed that a shroud lowered over us. The room we were shown was the most cramped I have ever seen. I have since rented larger areas just to store paintings. The entire room we were given was, I would say, eight feet by six at most. It had a single bed, one tiny chest of drawers, a mirror, a small sink, and a sepia photograph of family ancestry. The only window was the size of a small book. I still wonder why anyone would bother making a window so small.

In contrast, the owner of the house was a giant. A Bavarian housefrau with a well-developed mustache and a massive hulk of a body atop two stocking-clad tree-trunk legs. An awesome wreck of a woman. There was not the slightest evidence that she had ever smiled.

"Can we see the other room," I asked, still holding out hope.

"No ozzere room," she hissed. "Zis is for you. It is *sehr gut*, no? Yes?"

"It's very nice!" I tried to smile at the lady. "But I don't think it's quite enough for two. Unless one of us sleeps on the floor!"

This produced an indignant grunt from the hideous mustached lips. Hans and she launched into serious dialogue.

"Vell, it iz all zat ve can profide for ze moment," he said. "You vill make it very kozi I zink."

It was a fait accompli. We were officially tenants. She handed us two backdoor keys, along with a stern admonishment: no parties, no smoking, no noise.

How in the name of all that's holy would we have a party in an eight by six room? I left it alone.

Hans then extended his kindness to the breaking point, inviting us to his house for lunch. What he didn't tell us is that we would be obliged to eat in the kitchen with the maid. Lunch consisted of black bread, coffee warmed up from breakfast, and some sort of brown goo that neither Ruth nor I could identify.

What the meal lacked in presentation and nutrition it made up for in staying power. I tasted it for the next three days.

31
The Derailed Train

At some point, many years before, our Bavarian landlady had been young. No doubt she'd had a mum and dad who loved her. She would have had a favorite teddy bear and a special dress for holidays. She would have flirted with the little boy next door and run and skipped through the fields of long summer grass with the other children. Probably she would have had birthday parties and sticky buns and wanted to know how the moon worked.

Somewhere along the line the train went off the tracks.

Years passed. Life twisted and turned, molding her into a monolithic matriarch, a towering fortress of granite, impenetrable and frigid.

She ran her world like a demented tyrant, basing everything upon a rigid routine from which she never varied. Everything was done in strict accord with her timetable.

She made it clear from the outset that there would be no pleasantries. She did not relish our presence in her home. We were there on sufferance. No smoking within fifty feet of the house; no entry after eight o'clock; above all no noise of any kind, at any hour.

We lived on tiptoe.

Her daily routine did not vary. She rose long before the sun and began work in her kitchen. There she boiled large cauldrons of meat that she allowed to simmer for the entire day. Accompanied by large slices of the local black bread, this meat made up her evening meal. After who knows how many decades of this routine, the entire house was impregnated with a decaying aroma reminding one of an abattoir or glue factory. Most mornings, Ruth and I dressed and ate as quickly as possible to get out into the fresh air. Our breakfast, invariably, was black bread and instant coffee. Wasting no time, we hauled our instruments to Hans and Gretel's home for the daily session.

Gretel was responsible for our German elocution. She was to teach us the correct pronunciation and inflection for the lyrics of the songs we were learning. We didn't do well. German is a difficult language to learn in the best of situations. It's even more difficult when studying with an ill-equipped teacher. She had no patience whatsoever and barraged us with unrelenting sarcasm. I suppose it was her idea of humour, but it was counterproductive.

Ruth and she formed an immediate mutual hatred. This perhaps could have been anticipated. Ruth, after all, was slender and beautiful. Many women hated her at first sight. The ongoing antagonism created a mental block in Ruth's learning ability. Eventually, she developed a flawless German accent and passed as a native in certain brief circumstances. During our month of study, however, Ruth froze.

One afternoon, Gretel locked Ruth in a tiny room of the studio, threatening to keep her captive until she learned at least one of the required songs. Ruth stomped back and forth, enraged. Then, to her immense credit, she collected herself and sat down to memorize the lyrics. On the next take she had them perfectly.

32
Strandgut

L earning those six songs became a challenge that we decided to embrace. No matter what, we would meet it
with the fortitude shown by those brave souls on the
beaches of Normandy.

Within a month, we were able to sing six songs in passable
German. As a reward, we were reinstated in the regal splendour
of our original hotel, after a month of hell in the eight-foot square
cell. We again were able to shower and swing our arms without smacking each other.

We had no idea what the lyrics meant, but that didn't seem
to bother our producers. Of course, we didn't bring it up. Any
questioning or hesitation on our part might have meant returning to the eight-foot square.

We made an album named *Strandgut*. In German this means
"flotsam" (as in flotsam and jetsam, material washed up on the
beach). Ironically, Webster's also defines flotsam as "vagrant
impoverished people." This quite aptly described us at the time.

The album's cover featured Ruth and me standing waist-
deep in what was supposed to be the Mediterranean. During
the day-long January photo shoot, which took place in the freezing Atlantic, we absolutely ruined our new Mic Mac attire. We
had bought two very expensive outfits specially for the event.

Do you think we were reimbursed for them?
No one had ever made an album like *Strandgut*. Unfortunately, no one has ever heard it — at least not as we made it. Let me explain.

We found out later that the recording studio to which we were taken produced an endless supply of "elevator music" albums. These mindless collections of popular music were usually assembled by disenchanted producers assisted by hack musicians who would otherwise be driving trucks. In fact, the albums were put together much like trucks — by formula and assembly line. The producer tried to duplicate exactly what had worked before, with as little variation as possible. The final product was then fed into the commercial pipeline to be unleashed on unsuspecting shoppers, hotel guests, and prison inmates across the length and breadth of Europe.

Our recording session was to be squeezed in for a day or two between these formula albums, with as little inconvenience to the real work on hand as possible.

We arrived at the recording studio, a vast room the size of a basketball arena, where we dutifully ("and as quickly as possible pleez") sang the fourteen songs per instruction. Everything came out better than we had expected, including the six songs in German. We recorded everything in three days. Most songs we hit right in just one or two takes. The pace was breathtaking.

After the final number was declared a take, we were allowed into the inner sanctum of the recording booth, where the engineer was on his twelfth schnapps of the day. It was, after all, nearly lunch time.

The quality of our voices pleasantly surprised us when played through the huge speakers. Thick spools of recording tape looped slowly through the equipment, and out came the two song birds clear as a bell.

This was state-of-the-art stuff then. Eight-track recording was just coming into its own. We were on the vanguard. The last time I checked, recording equipment had become digital, offering a potentially infinite number of tracks. That's progress, I suppose. Before long, recording companies will dispense with singers altogether. Some people might offer the opinion that they already have.

We left feeling pleased with ourselves. Hans told us that we would need to return for some overdubbing the following week, but he assured us it would take no more than an hour or so.

All that would then remain would be to print the album with a well-chosen photo of the two love birds on the cover. The distribution company would quickly get it into the stores, and we would wait for the royalty checks to show up in the mail.

The following week, when we arrived for the dubbing, they played the album for us. The most bizarre collection of sounds either of us had ever heard squawked through the speakers. In our absence, they had added to our voices and our two steel folk guitars a collection of what they euphemistically called "orchestrations." They had used just about every instrument known, including harp, woodwinds, brass and horn, and even an enormous Chinese gong imported from a nearby temple. In so doing, they had effectively reduced our singing to background vocals.

The result was the most alarming example of raucous musical destruction imaginable. Quality had become secondary. Hans assured us that since we knew nothing about the commercial side of music, we shouldn't worry. He guaranteed us that the album would be an enormous hit and that very soon we would all be rich.

Ruth and I knew differently. We had become instant elevator music, not to be taken seriously by anyone interested in the type of music we sang.

It was over. We had put our trust in this collection of besotted recording gangsters and had, quite predictably, been party to a collection of utter rubbish. We stood outside the studio on a cold, bleak Munich afternoon with little more in our pockets than when we had arrived. We had two dilapidated guitars, some loose change, and an experience we would no doubt be able to laugh at in about twenty years.

Twenty years and more have passed. I'm still not laughing.

33

Studio B Toilet Rolls

We had come a long way from busking on the Riviera, but we had little to show for it. The studio didn't release our album. They sat on it. We waited, then asked about it, then begged. Nothing we said or did could induce them to put our work on the stands.

Essentially they told us, "Thank you very much, you're free to go." Right. As long as we didn't record for anyone else — specifically for a company that understood us and truly wanted to work with us to produce quality, salable music.

And go where? We were next to penniless in Munich. February was coming on hard. The wind seemed to spit snow, and we had few prospects.

Ever resourceful, we visited a few local clubs. On the strength of at least having recorded an album, we got auditions for gigs. To our relief, once we started contacting club owners, we had no trouble getting work. Bragging aside, we were getting pretty damn good by then. We'd certainly had our share of experience. My guitar work had improved considerably, as had my voice. Ruth was, as always, the consummate professional. Then, too, we were English. With the Beatles riding their crest, an English duo went over well. We found a much better reception in Germany, I feel, than we would have in England.

We played in Munich clubs two or three nights a week and on weekends. The money was paltry but steady, and we moved into a rundown little place near the wrong side of town.

One consolation was that we were able to devote time during the days to our art. We had a set of songs that we knew backward and forward (six in German, you may recall), so we didn't have to spend even a moment in practice.

At that point, we didn't care. We played the clubs, we were appreciated, we were paid. Our bills were covered, so we spent our mornings and afternoons drawing and painting.

I bought a set of oils, some canvas, and two cheap easels. Our digs weren't conducive to sculpture, so Ruth too dived into painting. We visited museums, galleries, and after a few weeks even placed a few pieces on exhibition. Germany was turning out to be a good locale for us.

A month or so later, as March ran its course, a hip-looking guy came backstage after one of our shows. He was a very flashy dresser, quite a dashing figure. It turned out that he was heir to an optical manufacturing fortune. With his spare money, he dabbled in the arts. He loved our act and asked if he could be our agent. We never got around to signing a contract with him, but he represented us and started booking us around Munich and nearby cities. He helped us get a more upscale apartment and started to make things happen.

He always bought American cars. He had them imported and drove them like calling cards. He lent us one of his castoffs, and we began to feel that things were moving ahead for the first time in quite awhile.

A month and a half later, it was early spring and the recording company still had not brought out our album. We'd given up on it, but were still stuck in the horrendous ten-year contract. Our agent, who was doing well by us, advised us to let it go for the time being and see how things worked out. That was sensible, since there was hardly an alternative.

One weekend, our agent flew to Berlin on family business. Traveling first class, he got to talking with the person in the seat next to him. The man turned out to be Chris Howland, a very pleasant and personable Englishman. Chris had been posted to Germany shortly after the war to anchor a radio program for British troops still stationed abroad. The show had enjoyed instant success and had catapulted Chris to fame. He settled in Germany, milking his success, and ultimately secured his own television show, syndicated throughout Germany and surrounding countries.

Chris's show was the place to tune in the top ten. It was similar to the Dick Clark Show in the States, and was widely popular among many age groups.

Our agent secured a live booking for us on the show. Apparently he had talked us up on the plane, and upon returning to Munich had immediately sent Chris tapes of our album.

This was quite a coup, a real blockbuster. We prepared wholeheartedly, knowing that such exposure could launch us.

Chris Howland had the reputation of being a relaxed, easygoing sort of fellow. One got the impression that a bomb could go off next to him and it would hardly ruffle his casual charm and smooth delivery.

As is often the case, the opposite was true. He invariably got the most frightful attack of nerves before going on air. This is not uncommon among performers, even the most experienced. Each seems affected in his or her own way. In Chris's case, it manifested as acute diarrhea. He usually had to take a run to the men's room half an hour or so before showtime.

The night Ruth and I were to appear, the network was trying out the newest form of wireless microphone — the kind that clips onto the clothing to allow free movement anywhere on the set. The usual break in pre-show setup was called right on time, half an hour before the show started. Off the nervous emcee trotted to the toilet, but in his haste he forgot to turn off the mike, which was still attached to his shirt.

The entire studio was treated to the sounds of the show's star relieving himself in Super Surround Sound. It gave the event a veritable Philharmonic feel. Some bright technician had the presence of mind to tape the entire proceedings. He played it back when Chris returned to the set. To his credit, Chris took it in the spirit of a veteran performer. Thank God there had been no audience.

The show went exceptionally well. Ruth and I were in top form. Our harmonies were resonant and our selection of songs seemed perfect. Immediately after we came off stage, a little man trotted up to us and introduced himself as an A&R executive from our recording company. "What are you doing here?" we asked, amazed that the company would take any interest in us. "Haven't you heard? We're about to release your album." I didn't know whether to kiss him or punch him in the nose. Those ungrateful bastards. They had done nothing for months. Then, when through our own efforts we got booked on a big TV show, they jumped on our bandwagon.

We spoke with him for a minute or two, then headed back to our flat. It may have been wisdom, or complete disgust, but we simply took it in stride. At that point, we were about one week from flat broke. The recording company had given us nothing, and we didn't intend to start counting on anything from them in the future.

When we got back to our apartment, I had the urge for a little toilet activity of my own. Nature took its course, but at the critical point I found that we had run out of toilet paper. I don't know why I fail to check such important accouterments before seating myself. After using a few sheets from the phone book, I emerged relatively unscathed, but seething. Somehow the whole thing epitomised our precarious condition.

"I'm gathering up our empty bottles and cashing them in for some bloody bog paper," I shouted to Ruth. Broke or not, I refused to take another crap without having something to wipe with.

I stormed over to the supermarket and cashed in fifty-seven pfennigs worth of bottles. The store had a giant display of toilet paper, offering two choices. You could economise and choose the generic sandpaper variety, or go whole hog and take the super-duper softy.

I was leaning toward buying the cheaper brand and investing the remainder in a chocolate bar, which would be our dinner, when three teenage girls came giggling up to me. They had seen me on TV — and could they please have my autograph!

Fame struck in front of the toilet roll display.

34
Bubblegum Rock

To our utter disappointment, when the album was released, the critics deemed it bubblegum music. This
meant that it was thought fit mostly for preteens and
other mental pubescents. The German term for this type of
music was *Schlager*, loosely translated as popular hit music.

We had started our careers as folk musicians, with the goal
of saving the world through song. We had emerged the darlings of eleven- and twelve-year old children, whose primary
goals in life were hiding their acne and trying not to walk into
walls when members of the opposite sex were around.

In frustration, I overstate the situation. Our fans ranged
through many age groups, as the word *Schlager* implies. A song
from the album, "Mr. Akkermann," went into the German top
forty. We had sung it in German, and to our surprise it became
known throughout the country. Believe me, nothing could be
stranger than turning on the radio and hearing yourself singing in German.

The song had been written by Hans's wife, Gretel, who constantly threatened to cut off his matrimonial nookie if he didn't
record at least one of her songs. He probably saw the recording
of our album as the perfect time to toss it in with the mix, thinking it would never be heard from again.

"Mr. Akkermann" was the musical rendition of a conversation between a German businessman and his mistress. She calls while he's in an important business meeting. He keeps joking with her, pretending that she is a Mr. Akker-mann, a business associate. Finally she releases the punch line, saying, "The real joke arrives in March."

How such a song could get into the top forty is beyond me. Perhaps our accents were so bad no one could understand the meaning. Or else, as I would rather believe, our voices and harmonies transcended the meaning. Listening to the song years later, I had to admit that it hit the mark. I could see how people were fascinated. Ruth's voice was fetching and coquettish. The back and forth between us was lively. And, of course, the undercurrent was highly sexual.

We became so well known after the album was released that for a time we couldn't go out without attracting a crowd. Once we were surrounded by admiring fans and signed autographs for over an hour at the Blumenmarket, surrounded by towering displays of fresh flowers. We did a Radio Free Europe tour, composed and performed music for several films, and generally had a high old time.

Through it all we hardly made a pfennig. Not that we were naive and let money slip through our fingers. By then we had gotten quite savvy. It's just that musical fame is ephemeral: it's difficult to pin down the money. Our recording company, for example, continually told us that they had not yet reached the break-even level for our album, even though the single had shot up on the charts. Expenses for travel ate into profits from our shows, and we never quite got into that elusive area where enough money is made to start saving.

Our agent decided to go back to his family business. We could hardly blame him. I can imagine how excited his wealthy father must have been to have his son traipsing around the country with a couple of foreign musicians.

35

Swan Song

Fortunately, while we were still surfing on the Chris Howland wave, our agent had booked us for a second tour. It was outstandingly successful. We made thirteen appearances around the country, and the German locals loved us. Our album and top-40 single were still recent news. The auditoriums were usually sold out. There's nothing quite like three encores for soothing one's ailments!

The newspapers went out of their way to praise us. The following is an excerpt from a paper in Berlin:

> With her long chestnut hair she looks equally provocative in an evening dress or miniskirt. After only a few moments her voice and presence had captivated the audience. Ruth Roberts, sculptress from the USA, is quickly becoming established in her new career. Kerry Hallam, painter from England, his long legs moving to the rhythm and speaking in a touching, broken German dialogue, is more than just a sidekick. He is Ruth's partner, M.C. and comedian.
>
> Kerry and Ruth met in a small village in the South of France. One of their original ballads tells of this romantic meeting in St. Tropez. Their first LP was recently released, and Ester and Abi Ofarim will soon be finding competition!

The charming Ruth and her partner Kerry, with his dry wit, have a natural spontaneity. Each plays a guitar, each sings, and their music ranges from traditional folk and modern ballads to their own compositions and musical clownery.

The audience was delighted and joined in on several of their songs. Ruth and Kerry were not allowed to leave before singing two encores and promising to return again very soon.

Unforseen good fortune struck us on the tour. After our concert in Frankfurt, a little goat of a man in an expensive suit came backstage and introduced himself. He told us that he was a lawyer — and a devoted fan.

When we got to talking, Ruth mentioned something about how unhappy we were with our recording contract. He asked us a few questions and agreed that we'd gotten the short end of the stick.

It turned out that this short, nondescript fellow was a powerful and highly sought-after lawyers in the country. He practiced in three countries — Germany, England, and France — and was known as an absolutely brilliant attorney.

Next afternoon, we stopped into his office. He made a call for us to our producers. We listened in on his speakerphone, and it was one of the most astounding conversations I've ever heard. Hans and the other executives were petrified. They hardly spoke three sentences.

That was it! Our contract was dissolved.

Our company even agreed to pay us two thousand marks in severance. It was a pittance, about five hundred dollars at the time, but it was an added bonus nonetheless considering that we would have been glad to pay to get away from them.

Flying from Stuttgart to Berlin on Pan Am for the final leg of our concert tour, we were met at the airport by a bustling welcoming committee from "Amerika Haus," under whose auspices our concert was being presented.

The Amerika Haus had a sparkling history. After the war, the United States, like any self-respecting victorious nation, decided to enlighten the vanquished by bringing them up to the cultural and social mores of their conquerors. Toward that end, the U.S. opened cultural centers in most of the major cities throughout Germany, at which lectures, concerts, and workshops were offered at little charge. By the time of our arrival, these centers had enjoyed great success for twenty years and had become part of the social fabric of the new Germany.

After arriving, we stood around with the welcoming members, waiting for our baggage to arrive on the carousel. It finally appeared and was dutifully removed and taken by a burly driver to the waiting car. Our two guitars, however, did not show up. We were assured by the beaming Pan Am desk attendants that the airline had probably given them special handling.

Fifteen minutes later, we started to worry. More reassurances from Pan Am. No need to be concerned, we were told. Whenever someone in any kind of official capacity tells me not to worry, that is the signal for me to do precisely that.

Another ten minutes passed. Still no instruments. Lots of nods and smiles from the Pan Am counter, however.

"I don't like the look of this," I told the Amerika Haus contingent. "They've obviously lost the damn things, and our concert starts in two hours. I'm going to have a word with someone."

By now the terminal had thinned considerably. Almost all passengers from our flight had retrieved their luggage and were on their way home. I marched to the Pan Am desk and asked the smiling lady if she would please find someone in authority to help with this very serious problem.

After what seemed an age, a young man in Pan Am uniform came out to the desk. In ponderous and comforting tones he assured me that everything was under control, and that there was no need to be concerned. The instruments would arrive-eventually.

"Eventually!" I screamed. "What in God's good name does that mean? Where the hell are they?"

'Well, Sir, dis is zer embarazzing. Ein fact, ze inztruments are eizer en rote to Zan Frazisco or Paris." Having at last broken down to honesty, he hung his head with the servility of a schoolboy caught cheating at midterm.

I counted to twenty. Then counted again.

A cloud settled over our group, which passed the next ten or fifteen minutes with worried brows, bowed heads, and shuffling feet. Finally, Ruth and I went to have coffee, leaving the Amerika Haus people huddled with the airline representatives at the Pan Am counter.

Not ten minutes later, one of the Pan Am gentlemen came running up to us. He had a "zolution." They would take us to a very reputable music store and rent two guitars for us. They realized that these would in no way replace our own precious instruments, but perhaps we would consider trying to make do, if only for the sake of the hundreds of people who would be disappointed should the concert not take place.

We tried to be gracious. It was very kind of him, we explained. But we were sure that he would understand: instruments are very personal items. Ours were of professional quality, made specifically to our requirements, immensely valuable, irreplaceable, etc. (Our budgets really didn't run to more than ordinary guitars. Of the two, Ruth's Favella was far better than my old Stella, which should have been splintered for firewood long before. We had become accustomed to making do.)

After whispered debate, our hosts begged us at least to try a few of the instruments. It wasn't asking too much, surely? They were so imploring that we finally had to agree. Delighted, they promptly whisked us off to the music shop.

What we saw brought tears to our eyes: row after row of high-end guitars hanging in silent splendor. Glistening strings. Lush mahogany and finely sculpted pine bodies.

We settled for two Martin D28's (undoubtedly one of the finest models that distinguished company has produced). Strumming in delight, we assured the airline people that we would do our level best to manage, troopers that we were. Everyone had to understand, however, that at best this would be makeshift.

We could hardly wait to get to the theater for our sound check. Entering a magnificent location, we found the acoustics superb. The two Martins sounded like celestial organs. The sound was rich, velvet, and balanced. We had never played such aristocratic instruments. Our rehearsal ran much longer than usual, so exquisite was the sound. We felt that this would be a concert to end all concerts. Thank God for the ineptitude of Pan Am.

Half an hour before curtain, a young man in Pan Am uniform rushed backstage. Drenched in sweat, he breathlessly informed us that our guitars had been found. They were waiting in his van outside, and could we please carry them in? He would have brought them inside himself, he said, but his superiors had informed him that they were far too valuable and that only we should handle them. If we would be so kind as to carry in the irreplaceable jewels, he said, he would take back the shoddy replacements.

Ruth and I glanced at each other, shaking our heads. It had been too good to be true. I recall that we were called back for three encores that evening. Had we been able to retain the Martins, who knows how many more we would have rated?

36
The Rise and Fall of Our
Only Album

B ack in Munich after the tour, we were astounded to find that we had hardly enough money to last us through the month. We didn't know if the problem was with our method of booking, our fees, or our financial ineptness.

All we knew was that, in spite of arriving fresh from a triumphant tour, we immediately would have to go back on the road. With this realization, our musical ambitions seemed pointless. If all this work led to nothing, we thought, we might as well go someplace nice and starve. What was holding us? We were out of our contract. We had no obligations. We were our own bosses again. The only trouble is that we were at square one financially. We wanted only to run, to be anywhere but Munich.

Without an agent, we tried the local clubs. It was a slog, but we got a few gigs and kept food on the table.

I feel that our reception by the clubs at that point was limited by the way our recording company had misrepresented us with their arrangement of songs. We were folk musicians, nothing more and nothing less. When we appeared in concert, people responded to us enthusiastically. A club atmosphere demands something different, something more showy. The two of us sitting on stage, with just our voices and guitars, had trouble fulfilling expectations of audiences coming to us because of an album overflowing with Bavarian orchestra music. We had a style and a degree of integrity that we felt we needed to maintain. We believed that if we gave that up, we had no chance of making it. We never tried to give anyone the impression, and we certainly were under no illusion, that we were anything more than a folk singing duo. Some responded to that, others did not. The club owners, however, continually demanded lavish stage performances in the styles of Sinatra, Garland, or Pat Boone.

Years after the fact, Ruth and I discussed the probabilities of what had happened during our "discovery." We now feel that when Hans saw us in St. Tropez, he had truly thought of us as potentially successful singers. A few years before meeting us, he had represented an exceptionally popular male-female singing duo. They were a polished act well known throughout Germany.

One way or another, they had gotten out of their contract and had flown Hans's coup. When he came across Ruth and me in St. Tropez, he saw the possibility of developing a similar act. He called the top dogs of the company down for a look. They arrived quickly. And no wonder. Who wouldn't leave Germany for an all-expenses paid trip to St. Tropez?

Once Ruth and I arrived in Germany, the top dogs of the company introduced us to the top-top dogs, who handed us over to the top of the top-top dogs. They immediately saw that we were an act entirely unlike Han's former duo. We were relatively unpolished folk performers who spoke no German, preferring to sing obscure American folk songs that hardly anyone in Germany appreciated.

As Ruth and I have since surmised, the company most likely decided to go ahead with the recording because they felt they had little to lose. They realized that they could at least write the whole thing off (including their original trips to St. Tropez). They would then sit on the album, having it ready should anything positive happen in our favor. This eventually came about in the form of the Chris Howland Show.

It seems that the executives hedged even further by recording us as essentially background vocals to a Bavarian orchestra. That style of musical arrangement gave the company the ultimate option of simply dropping the tracks that had our voices. They would then have an album of elevator music that they could hock to any number of sources.

Talk about getting the shaft!

The album gradually died. Our single slipped from the charts, and our triumphant tour became a memory. Back in Munich, we began shuffling from tenuous gig to tenuous gig. At a party, Ruth and I were introduced to a lovely woman who owned a small nightclub in Schwabing, the bohemian district of Munich. She invited us to do a couple of nights on the weekends, and we moved into a small flat in Elizabeth Strasse and made her booking our bread and butter. We were tired and needed a break. Ruth especially was feeling the strain of late nights and ongoing financial pressure.

At the time, I was reading William Shirer's book *The Rise and Fall of the Third Reich*. It was so fascinating I could hardly put it down. Living in the country in which it all took place lent a compelling reality to the entire story, so much that my imagination began to get the better of me.

One cold spring morning, I was returning to our flat with a bag of groceries in my arms. Turning a corner, I came face to face with two Nazi SS officers in full uniform. I stopped dead in my tracks. They seemed to eye me suspiciously as they smoked their cigarettes.

With the Shirer book very much in mind, my first inclination was to turn and run. This was 1967, however, not 1939. What were these Nazis doing on a main street at ten o'clock in the morning? I eased past them, trying not to look disturbed.

Only after, when I was well down the street, did I realize that a large film studio had its lot and studios nearby. These SS officers were actors taking a smoking break! The episode was disconcerting, however. Especially when the Neo-Nazi Party polled five per cent of the Bundestag a few weeks later.

37
Escape

One morning, whilst we were counting our pfennigs and finding that, as usual, we were in a rather dilapidated financial condition, the phone rang. It was the producer of a film being made for German TV. He apologized for even calling, saying that he realized we were probably booked solid because we were so famous. If, however, we could manage to squeeze a few moments from our busy schedule, he would love to get together and tell us about his latest film production, for which he needed a score.

It's difficult to maintain dignity when one is on the bread line. However, there are certain rules that have to be followed in this kind of situation. With great composure, and in the most casual tone I could muster, I told him that we were, in fact, extremely over committed. Could he perhaps call back in the morning?

Since we were absolutely broke, I can assure you that putting him off took some balls. We managed to hang on to our sanity through the night. He called midmorning, just as we had started to think that we had played it a little too close. We told him that we would love to get together that very afternoon. Not that we could promise anything, mind you, but it just might be possible to rearrange our hectic schedule.

By judicious use of bus, train, and foot, we managed to get within an affordable taxi ride of the producer's office. We scraped together enough for cab fare, allowing us to arrive in a relatively impressive fashion as real stars, not down-and-outs. Once at our destination, we lingered while paying the cabbie, taking plenty of time so our hosts could see us arriving in style.

Inside the rather modest offices, we went through the usual to-ing and fro-ing and finally agreed, since this was simply a "fill in," on a price for our services. We even managed to get some cash up front. Ah, the sweet thrill of it all!

The little epic movie was not destined to be a contender at Cannes, but it served to facilitate our escape from the clutches of the great unwashed. We had been in Germany for nearly six months. We had managed to survive the winter and the great recording fiasco. We had made some new friends and played one or two good gigs, but it was time to move on.

We had followed a dust cart thinking it was a wedding.

38

Milk Pipeline

The TV film took us out of Germany and into Switzerland, one country closer to St. Tropez. Travelling with the producer, editor, and actors, we proceeded by train through winding gorges and across flower-strewn mountain meadows.

The crew set up shop in Fanas, a village of perhaps four hundred residents high in the Alps. When we arrived, spring was in first bloom. In those high Alpine pastures, spring and summer are relegated to the months of June, July, and August. Perhaps as a result, the charm of the days and nights is more concentrated and pleasurable than in the lowlands. Wild mountain flowers scented the air. The slow, muffled clang of cowbells tumbled slowly down the slopes. Farmers prepared fields for the year's crops. Enormous clouds floated past, close enough to reach out and touch.

The film's producers, who had thought that Fanas's residents would be delighted to appear as extras, were shocked when not a single resident turned out for the first day's filming. Signs were put up and the word went out: Extras Welcome! No response. More signs were put up and more words went out — extras were not only welcome, they were needed! Nothing.

After discreet questioning of town officials (and a strategic afternoon spent in the local tavern to check the pulse of the village), the producers had to conclude that the film crew was viewed with great suspicion among the rather narrow and provincial locals.

A few days passed. Nothing changed, yet the film could not be shot without local actors. The plot revolved around an important event that had been planned in the area for some time. At those altitudes, the best grazing area for cows was often several thousand feet or more above the villages, on the sunny grassy slopes near the mountaintops. This brought up a logistical difficulty: how did the farmers get the milk to the villages for processing and bottling? Did they herd the somewhat slow and decidedly unagile creatures half a mile or more down steep slopes to the stables for milking every day, and then herd them back up afterward? Or did they milk the cows right on the slopes, then carry down the heavy containers of milk?

Neither solution had proved practicable, so a group of young men and women were circulating among the villages in the region building long plastic tubes, or milk pipelines. "Die Milch Pipeline" would allow farmers simply to pour the milk into the tubes, allowing gravity to do its work.

The construction of the milk pipeline had been set up for the village of Fanas months before. The film crew hoped to capture the unusual event, throwing in a loosely knit plot of love between a travelling worker and a local villager. But the film needed extras, and the locals remained elusive.

Then Ruth and I had an idea. We volunteered to give a concert, free to all comers, in hopes that it would bring the community together. Arrangements were made and announcements went out. Two nights later, the local auditorium was packed. Even the village elders, who had most vehemently shunned the visiting crew, attended eagerly.

The evening could not have gone better. An absolute smash. The tiny village had never heard nor seen anything like it. The following morning, over a hundred villagers turned out for the filming. The elders, of course, pushed to the front, all of a sudden anxious for film immortality.

Ruth and I wrote the score for the film and recorded it on the spot. It was easy work. We started early each day and ended by mid-afternoon. This gave us plenty of time to climb through the hills and paint the little villages, each like a picture postcard. We spent ten luxurious days in those beautiful surroundings, writing and recording the soundtrack in the morning, painting in the afternoon.

When the film ended, the last thing we wanted was to return to Germany. We had nothing lined up there. Just thinking about it was depressing. Almost at the same moment, we thought, "Let's go back to where it all started. To the sun, to where we were successful before."

We hopped a train in Zurich, and the next day we were in St. Tropez.

It was as though we had never left. We luxuriated in the familiar surroundings. It was like coming home. In no time we re-established our connections with the restaurants and were back in the old routine of busking. It was refreshing to the utmost. We both felt born again.

Busking is eminently simple. You sing. You pass the hat. You take the tips and spend them! There is none of the rather nasty business that seems to go hand in glove with "serious" entertaining. No contracts, no one promising you the world and tossing a net over you. No one siphoning off your money.

It was clear to us that our friends had been right. We had bitten off more than we could chew. We had run before we walked, had bought the seductive hype, and had ended up flat on our arses.

Not to worry. We were back in our old stomping grounds.

We spent some of the film money on a Deux Chevaux that fit the bill perfectly. We moved into a charming little place, right on the main street of Ramatuelle. It was one large room that had two beds, a small living area, and a more-than-adequate kitchen. Almost every afternoon we'd buy freshly baked crusty French bread (absolutely the best on earth), salad makings, a bottle of wine, and two big filet mignons. Wine was so cheap then in France it was almost free. Ruth would fix a mouth-watering meal, and we'd open up the front doors and eat while watching the town walk by. After dinner we'd pack up our guitars and head off to our evening busking. A hot meal like that always put us in good stead.

One day I walked unsuspectingly into a record store and heard playing on the music system one of the original songs that had been on our album. The title of the song was "Annie Love," one of our better pieces. I had written the music, and Michael Ashe, a close friend in London, had written the words. I walked to the counter and asked who the singer was.

Harry Belafonte?

I could hardly believe it. I just stood there and listened. The music was exactly as we had recorded it. Arrangement, background instrumentation — everything was practically unchanged. It sounded as though Belafonte's producers had simply removed my voice from the soundtrack and plugged in his.

"Annie Love" was the "A" side of his new single. This assured that it was likely to get a lot of air play. Belafonte was big stuff then. He'd had major hits in the recent past — "Day-O" ("Banana Boat Song"), among others.

I ran to a phone and called Michael Ashe, my co-writer. He'd heard nothing about it and was quite angry. He insisted that the recording company should have consulted with us, or even asked for our permission, before giving someone the right to one of our creations. He said that he'd look into it right away and get back to me. As information was uncovered, we learned that Belafonte's managers were trying to change his image from calypso to pop, in the hopes that he could become more mainstream. They apparently felt that our ballad was the vehicle.

Far from being upset, I was pleased. I saw it as an opportunity. Still, I took it with a grain of salt. I'd wait to spend the money till any checks arrived — and cleared.

Ruth and I began to put the winter in Germany behind us. Every morning we woke up and gazed into a blue, cloudless sky. We began to get back into the calm flow of Mediterranean life. As the season shifted into gear, St. Tropez was, as always, pure St. Tropez. Our summer looked as though it would be fabulous. With the dank and dreary days of winter and bratwurst behind us, how could things not be better?

39

Jean Marie

Café Des Arts was one of the finer restaurants we worked. The cafe's impresario, a middle-aged man named Jean Marie, was responsible for the nightly entertainment. Jean Marie was one of a kind. He was flamboyant and utterly eccentric — a true showman. Every night on the terrace outside the restaurant, he put together some type of bizarre entertainment for diners. The show was always improvised and spontaneous. More often than not, it was a total failure, but therein lay part of its charm. Jean Marie's forte was to provide the situation. It was up to the audience to get into the spirit of the thing.

One particularly memorable evening, a unicyclist joined Ruth and me on the bill. He put on a brilliant exhibition. While riding his unicycle among the tables and out onto the sidewalk and street, he held in his hands a separate bicycle handlebar and attached wheel. This gave the impression that he was riding a bicycle which could magically come apart at his whim. He would hurtle toward an unsuspecting car, and at the last second lift the front wheel out of the way and swerve aside on his unicycle.

People would gasp, amazed by the impossibility of the bike suddenly coming apart. It was a great act. Simply tremendous street performance.

That night, Jean Marie had installed on the terrace a large inflatable swimming pool filled with water. Two waiters dressed in Edwardian bathing suits were to stage a mock boxing match using large water cushions. About nine o'clock, when the restaurant was brimming with activity, Jean Marie stood before the crowd and grandly announced the commencement of the evening's entertainment. As he was about to introduce Ruth and me, a long Rolls Royce pulled slowly around the end of the terrace. It came to a sedate halt beside the swimming pool. The chauffeur hopped to and opened the back door. Out stepped an elderly dowager, dressed to the nines in the best that the Estate could buy. Holding a highly coiffured miniature poodle, the Grande Dame surveyed the scene with regal gaze.

Of course all eyes turned to the luxurious car and its fascinating occupant. Jean Marie's momentum had been interrupted. The unicyclist, sensing that the show was dragging, leaped into action. Picking up a head of steam, he raced hell for leather toward the unsuspecting dowager. While performing one of his more elaborate acrobatic feats, he impulsively lifted the lady and her poodle and tossed them with an enormous splash into the pool.

Time froze.

No one moved. Not a sound could be heard.

Jean Marie's face, grey at the best of times, turned ashen. Visions of lawsuits danced in his head. Gathering his wits, he rushed to help the poor woman and her poodle from the water.

She looked dreadful. Her hair, which she had undoubtedly worked on for hours, hung in wet dripping clumps. Her dress was ruined. Her poodle seemed none the worse off, but its careful coiffure of fluffy fur was matted tight, making it look like a large soggy rodent.

The unicyclist had taken cover around the corner, afraid even to watch what followed. The diners were well aware that this was not part of the evening's scheduled entertainment. Conversation was hushed. Everyone waited to see what would happen next. In shock, the drenched lady was led to the safety of the boutique above the restaurant.

Suspense mounted over the next hour. The sky darkened

and the moon rose. Everyone was dying to see how Jean Marie would extricate himself from this one. New diners arrived for their reservations, but tables were not available. No one wanted to leave.

About ten o'clock, the terrace lights dimmed and a crackling noise emitted from the café sound system. The static adjusted, and the bold strains of the British national anthem blared out loudly enough to be heard for miles.

The dowager emerged on the balcony above, wearing a Union Jack miniskirt, white patent leather boots, and a decollete blouse. She still held her poodle, which had been re-fluffed and decorated with enormous pink bows.

She descended the staircase, resplendent on the arm of Jean Marie, who shouted aloud to all who could hear that the lady had agreed not to sue.

The crowd gave the couple a hearty round of applause. She bowed and acknowledged the accolades as Jean Marie seated her.

Dinner for the lady and her guests was free that evening. Production costs can run a little high for improvisational theater. As the evening wound down, the dowager declared that she had not had so much fun since her husband had carelessly died some years before.

40

St. Tropez / Hey, Hey, Hey!

So there we were, surrounded on all sides by the delirious dance of St. Tropez in full season.

This exquisite little seaside town, once concerned only with fishing and the cork harvest, had been thrust into playing summer host to the jet set. Every sidewalk and restaurant was filled with the rich and famous, along with the aspiring rich and famous and the trainee rich and famous.

Being rich and famous is a tough business. Not only do you have to be rich and famous, you have to look rich and famous. There are several levels at work here.

The genuinely rich and famous couldn't care a rat's arse whether the world recognizes it or not. They usually want to escape prying eyes while vacationing. They get enough of that at home.

Those whose wealth and fame are questionable have a more difficult role. They often need to allay their own doubts by laboriously dressing the part. They continually have to make the effort to be seen in the right places with the right people. This results in a lot of elbowing and causes tension, sometimes making these people a drag to be with, even though they indeed might have a lot of money to spend.

Then there are the famous but not rich. These are rare birds, in a category on the edge. Many have to borrow to maintain an image, or to latch onto the rich but not famous who want to be seen with the famous but not rich.

Granted, it's a confusing subject.

Then there are the multitude of those in the invidious position of being rich but completely unknown. Included in this category would be, as an example, the pharmacist who owns ten retail outlets in Topeka. He might make a million and a half per year, but no one outside the local chamber of commerce knows it.

When people like this visit St. Tropez, they often have a real thirst for recognition. They'll sometimes go to any length to cozy up with the rich and famous or with the famous but not rich — or even with those whose fame and wealth are dubious.

There are various combinations of the above. All have one thing in common. They need to demonstrate that they are at least wearing the right uniform to play the game.

And what a game it is. A nonstop decathlon/marathon of seen and be seen in heated flux, from the nude beaches and dazzling soirees to the enormous yachts conveniently "parked" along the port so the owners can display their toys and lure unsuspecting prey up the gangplank.

Caution and decorum are thrown aside. Middle-aged London businessmen, who for fifty weeks of the year would die rather than loosen a necktie, are seen frolicking along the beaches in the briefest of bathing apparel-and quite often totally starkers.

Tycoons seek momentary diversion by hobnobbing with fellow fun-seekers who, under any other circumstance, would be persona non grata.

The young and the restless swarm beaches and nightclubs to rub shoulders with stars of film and stage. In certain circumstances, even the most rich and famous let down their hair and slither into a little discreet slumming.

Ferraris rub fenders with Mercedes and Rolls. And occasionally with a local Citröen.

In this atmosphere, boutiques thrive. Restaurants fill early. Night clubs flourish. Life is a carnival, a fascinating kaleidoscope of social intercourse. There are no constraints, no restrictions, no next-door neighbors passing judgment. Nothing curtails the pursuit of uninhibited hedonism.

Luxury is fundamental. Social mores are put on hold. It's fun and sun all the way. Accolades are bestowed on anyone who can come up with a more outrageous and inventive manifestation of *La Dolce Vita*.

Money is spent in torrents. That, and that alone, is mandatory.

Among these seekers of pleasure, Ruth and I wove our songs. Every evening was a saga. We were given outrageous tips. We were offered drinks and advances by strangers. One evening, a man whose name every reader of this story would recognize, took me aside and offered to buy Ruth for the night.

"She's not for sale," I told him.

"Just mention it to her, you might be surprised."

"I think not. With any luck, we'll both forget about this by morning."

I did mention it to Ruth several days later. She gagged, and we stayed all the closer together during our evenings of cheer.

41

In the Name of Progress

S t. Tropez had not always been such. The insanity fermented gradually, incrementally. I had seen it before. I have seen it since.

This is how it always seems to happen.

A group of artists, writers, and actors (which we'll call Group A) discovers and converges on a charming, unspoiled village.

The village is a place where they can live inexpensively, in relative calm, and enjoy their creativity far from constricting crowds. Most likely, the weather is fairly mild year round, with one outstanding season (winter or summer) that is glorious beyond imagination.

The artists and writers settle in, and for a time life is tranquil-and productive. But even artists have to buy food, for which they need to make money. They invite a client to stay for the weekend. The well-heeled outsider, who's richer than Rockefeller, is charmed by the little village and the artistic way of life. He (or she) buys a painting, and upon arriving back home tells a friend about the experience.

News travels fast. Before you can say Donald Trump, the sanctuary is invaded. More clients arrive, not to buy but to smell the turpentine, to watch the marble chips fly, to listen to the typewriters, and to join in "artistic" late night debates in the local café.

This is the second group. Wealthy patrons. Group B.
They have nothing much to show for a life of wheeling and
dealing-except enormous wealth. They are generally bored with
their daily lot. Adding zeros to their bank balances is all they
can look forward to.

The artists provide them with much-needed stimuli, with
a feeling of zest for life. It's exciting to be around people who
are real, who care about something other than the stock market.

The artists are tolerant at first. After all, what's wrong with
letting someone buy you dinner and a bottle of good wine? All
the person wants in exchange is a few exaggerated stories about
orgies. The wine flows. A few paintings are sold. Life is good.

Everyone gets what they came for.

Enter Group C.

The pretend artists. Those with no money, no talent, and
no real life. This group, hearing from friends about paradise,
decides to join the dance. They hope desperately that some of
the talent of Group A will rub off.

However, the effect is to dilute and diminish. Suddenly it's
hard to tell the original from the copy, hard to distinguish that
which is genuine from that which is contrived.

For a brief period, Groups A, B, and C mill around together,
trying not to tread on each other's toes. By this time, the output of Group A is deteriorating. There are too many demands,
too many meetings, too much drinking at lunch. Creativity is
the casualty.

The locale has by now become "image." It's written up in a
trendy magazine as a beautiful location, an exotic collection of
people doing exhilarating, provocative things.

Then a movie star spends a month's holiday nearby. It's all
so lovely, and friends talk to friends. *People* magazine picks up
on it. An important film is made using the location as a backdrop.

That's it. That's all it takes.

Movie stars descend. Rock stars slither out from beneath
their rocks. The nearest airport is deluged with requests for
landings of private jets. Nightly rates at the local motel skyrocket.

Within a six-month period, the city council makes the main street one way and builds a parking lot. Then the worst of the worst happens. The first true jet set arrivals are spotted.

"Oh, isn't that . . . ?"

"Look, there's . . . ."

And suddenly every fourth car is a Mercedes or Jaguar, signaling that the real money has arrived. Movie and recording executives. Fortune 500 chairmen. Junk bond billionaires. The rich and famous. The rich and not famous. The famous and not rich.

It's heady wine. Ripe pickings for Group D. The real estate developers.

It's undemocratic and therefore a mortal sin to leave paradise in the hands of only a few. It must be shared. Not with the masses, of course, but with those fortunate enough to be able to pay for the square footage so expensively restricted by local building codes.

The process of development begins. Property values skyrocket. The local population is delighted to sell their small old family properties for enormous sums. They can finally do what they've been struggling to do all their lives-move someplace different.

Main street, already one-way, is widened. The café is now a restaurant, serving dinner on its newly built terrace. Old downtown buildings are gutted and renovated for office space. Into these spaces pop, what else, three or four real estate offices.

And so Group E makes its arrival.

The upper-middle class. Then the middle-middle class. Doctors, lawyers, bureaucrats, accountants, insurance agents, car salesman-all flock like gadarene swine to the altar of fashion. They drink toasts in their new estates, feeling that buying into this particular rock assures their social acceptance.

By this time, of course, Group A has long since departed. The real artists have moved on to pastures new.

No problem. Group B simply transfers patronage to Group C. After all, what's the difference? Group C looks like Group A, talks like Group A, has the same habits as Group A.

And Group B can't tell the difference anyway.

The village still has a degree of excitement. One can turn a blind eye to the seasonal overcrowding and to the declining quality of dinner at the local café (now a restaurant) which has quadrupled its prices. But what we have in reality is a shell with no kernel.

Finally, signaling the end, enter Group F. Large busloads of tourists with cameras and stretch pants.

The first hamburger shop opens. The café (now restaurant) is sold and reopened under a new, more international name. Parking meters are installed on main street. The new Rand McNally places the name of the village (now a small city) in type large enough to read.

Progress is complete. The village has been changed completely and forever. The few remaining locals walk sadly, remembering former times. Even Group B longs for the good old days.

Ironically, a few members of Group C start talking out of the sides of their mouths, complaining that things aren't like they used to be.

Why is it I don't feel sorry for them?

42

Escape Again

When our recording company found out that we had returned again to singing in the streets of St. Tropez, one of the top executives sent us a scathing letter. He told us that artists who had recorded with such a prestigious label should not "demean themselves" in such a way.

I felt like telling them to go straight to hell, but decided instead to forget the whole thing. Of course, we never heard from them again on the matter.

Our single had gone into the Top 40, and our album had been out for some time, but we had seen not a pfennig from either. That didn't stop the German equivalent of the IRS from inquiring about our tax status. The government obviously thought we were making a mint. I sent a letter to them through Hans. Nothing came of it, but as the season ended in St. Tropez, this was one more reason not to return to Germany.

I heard through my friend Michael Ashe that the Belafonte version of our song had gone exactly nowhere. Apparently, his career had taken a sudden turn for the worse, and Michael told me not to expect any money from royalties.

I hadn't been holding my breath.

Things in St. Tropez weren't all that they should have been, either. Autumn crept near, and we gradually came to the conclusion that busking was not as pleasurable as it had been. It was a younger person's game. Certainly the lifestyle was enjoyable, but it was too inconsistent. And as before it left us little real time to devote to our art.

As is true of most things, busking was not as simple as it seemed. We had to be in a different place every evening. We always had to be "on." It got tiring after a time to continually sniff things out in advance. The simplicity turned complex. The fun became work.

That second season in St. Tropez, we had much the same competition as the first, Manitas de Plata in particular. Then too, there was a fabulous Jamaican steel band that was outrageously loud. Much of our singing took place outside on verandas and terraces, and if we found ourselves next door to the steel band, we'd be drowned out and wouldn't make much money from tips.

Waking up one morning, Ruth started telling me about a dream she'd had in the night. "Not before me mornin' coffee," I said, stumbling to the kitchen. She padded right after me in her slippers, insistent on telling me all about it.

In her dream, we had been singing in a big barn in the United States. The crowd had been applauding like madmen. We were a smash.

Right, I thought. "How would you like your eggs, Luv?"

That evening, things were quiet at Chez Fernand. Only about half the tables were occupied, and those by conservative groups eating demurely. Monsieur Le Patron stood by the large charcoal grill doing his best to look calm. Evenings like this gave him gas. All those empty tables, *mon Dieu!*

"*Eh! Voila!*" he replied, sticking out his jaw for emphasis when I asked why the place was so empty. "*C'est la vie.* Sometimes it is thus. We 'av no control. *Ca va?*" He nodded to himself, blowing imaginary smoke through his lips. He had resigned himself.

Ruth and I decided to have a coffee and wait before starting our performance. The present crowd did not give the impression of being generous tippers. We waited, letting the place fill a little. We needed at least a couple of good groups to make our effort worthwhile.

It was a fine evening, though. The aroma of steaks and oregano sizzled on the grill, wafting gently upward to the lattice canopy. The breeze was warm, the temperature ideal, the air laced with perfumes of the summer night. After we finished our coffees, the patron turned down the recorded music on the sound system. That was our sign to begin.

We were not looking forward to it. The pickings would be slim. But by that time we had enough experience to know that the show, meaning us, must go on.

When one has sung a particular number several hundred times, there is a tendency for the rendition to become a little hackneyed. The set we presented certainly had that flavour. We didn't have much spark. Much of that could have been the crowd. The diners weren't even interested enough to notice that the canned music had ended and the live show had started.

We finished our set with the usual flourish and radiant smiles, and Ruth started to *fait la casket*. She moved among the tables with our customary felt top hat, to which she had strategically pinned a flower and a ten-franc note to encourage similar donations.

The far corner of the room was dimly lit. As I put away our guitars, I noticed that Ruth seemed to be talking with some people at a table in half shadow. Suddenly she let out a shriek and flung her arms round a tall, stocky fellow who had risen from his seat. The whoops and hugs continued so I hurried over to see what was going on.

It turned out that Ruth had met an old friend, Ray Gordon, who owned a tavern in Connecticut where Ruth had sung before coming to Europe. Ruth was beside herself. It was as though she had found a long-lost relative.

I was introduced and we all sat down. Ray was on a brief holiday in Europe and had decided to drop down to St. Tropez for the weekend. Over a round of rather fine cognac, Ruth filled him in on the events that had led us to singing in this particular restaurant nearly four thousand miles from where she and Ray had last known each other.

The evening wove its way through ongoing rounds of drinks, accompanied by delicious fresh-baked *tart aux pommes*. Ray and I took an instant liking to each other. He was genial, gracious, a genuine raconteur. By midnight, we were ready to call it an evening. Ruth was like a new person. She had caught up on the news from home, and seeing Ray had perked her up considerably.

We agreed to meet at his hotel for breakfast in the morning.

It was after eleven when he finally appeared, complaining bitterly about the devastating effects of the Riviera cuisine. There seemed little point in my disrupting things by pointing out that the bottle and a half of cognac we had consumed could perhaps be the culprit. After a couple of gallons of coffee and some delicious croissants, his demeanor improved. He and Ruth took up where they left off, catching up on the news from back in Connecticut.

When Ruth went off to the ladies' room, Ray started to ask me about our plans. He knew that the St. Tropez season was ending, and we would have to start looking for something new. I told him that we really hadn't given it much thought.

"Are you planning to return to London?" he asked.

"The truth is," I said, deciding to lay it on the line for him, "singing is really a means to an end. Ruth wants to get back to her sculpting, and I'd like to get back to my painting." I told him that we'd been on a mad roller coaster out of control. I described how we'd had a bad time of it at the hands of the German recording company and the whole of the commercial music industry. The experience had left a sour taste. "Anyway," I finally concluded, "the truth is we hadn't made any plans as yet."

Ray studied his coffee cup for a while. Then he smiled and said, "It's a shame things didn't work out. I can sympathize, but you have to put it behind you and move on. I think you two have a lot of talent. You have real potential if you can find someone to handle you properly.'"

Of course, we had always felt that.

"Here's what I have in mind," he said. "How would you like to come over and do a month's engagement at my tavern in Connecticut? Three nights a week. We'll give you full room and board, pick up the tab on your travel, and pay you three hundred dollars a week. Ruth would love to be home for a while, and you'd get to see a little of the colonies. Check if we're up to snuff, right?"

I had learned the hard way that in business, as in any game, one should never show one's feelings to the opposing player. I knew that I had to remain stoical, reflective. I had to give Ray the impression that his offer would be worth our casual consideration-if nothing better came along.

Instead I found myself blurting out, "Christ. What a deal! Are you serious?"

He said he was quite serious. He wanted us to inaugurate the new addition to his tavern: a large barn refurbished as a dinner theatre.

A barn? With a theatre? In the United States?

"I always knew you were a witch," I told Ruth when she returned to the table.

43
To the States

Brimming with hope, we landed in Boston. A limousine, replete with chauffeur, collected us and whisked us along the Massachusetts Turnpike. Ruth and I played rock and roll full blast on the radio, savoring the experience.

I arrived in the U.S. heavily loaded with preconceptions. I had, after all, been conditioned by years of Hollywood movies, gangsters, jazz, chewing gum, cowboys and Indians, sharp-finned Cadillacs, GI's, Levis, Jeeps, and photos of Manhattan skyscrapers.

I expected everything to be bigger than I had seen before, but nothing could have prepared me for the real thing. I felt dwarfed by the buildings, the freeways and overpasses, the harangue of radio stations, the fleets of cabs flying this way and that, and the constant barrage of billboards. Every conceivable space seemed used in a frantic effort to encourage trade.

I was captivated by the grandeur of it all. Everything seemed like a Hollywood set that would be taken down after I passed by. We sped along the interstate in total comfort. No bumps or rattles, no frazzled nerves. Relaxation in the rear of a limo: I had always known America would be like this.

The streamlined journey blended with jet lag. Drifting into

an untroubled sleep, I awoke as we reached our final destination, a small town in Connecticut with the rather uninspiring name of Plainville. We were greeted by two or three hundred of Ruth's relations (twenty or so, really, but exuberant), including her mum, dad, and brother.

Americans didn't appear that different from folks back in Europe. Of course, America had turned English into a foreign language. I caught the words, but the gist of the thought often eluded me. Understanding even normal conversation was a challenge, and I had plenty of opportunity. Everyone was more than happy to engage in chatter with The Limey. I was cute. I was fun. Everyone was thoroughly enjoying themselves.

It was fall in Connecticut. The best of seasons in New England. Warm, hazy days were filled with the perfume of wood smoke and the subtle chill of approaching winter. The majesty of dazzling reds and auburns in the maple forests attracted tourists from the world over.

We were a smash hit on the first night of our engagement at the Tavern of the Wild Geese, as Ray Gordon had named the refurbished barn that now housed an impressive dinner theatre. Our debut was a guaranteed success. At least seventy percent of the audience was made up of Ruth's relations and former fan club. They would have applauded if we had sung through our armpits.

In a matter of days, we realised that life in the United States would be more comfortable for us than back in England. Swinging London had lost its zip. For ten years it had been the Pied Piper of the Pop Culture, the headquarters of the New Age. The city had played host to a nonstop party, and it needed a break and several bottles of aspirin.

A few days after our arrival, Ray Gordon arranged for the head of the local immigration office to have dinner with us. Ruth and I sang a few songs, and the evening lapsed into jollity. Ms. Immigration, an attractive woman of about forty, was serious about her wine. As she quietly slid under the table, grasping the remains of a bottle of Ray's finest, it was agreed that I could be issued a "Green Card" the following day, without the encumbrance of a formal application.

Sure enough, within a week, I found myself the proud

owner of the magical card. I was a legal resident of the United States. The government issued me a Social Security number and a driving license. As a resident alien I couldn't vote, bear arms, or sit on a jury. I was, of course, allowed to pay taxes.

Ruth and I moved into a house that, by British standards, was a mansion. It had more bedrooms than we would ever need, a dishwasher, several toilets, and a large garden. Ray provided us with an enormous car and as much food as we could eat, plus a tidy monthly check. In exchange, we performed three nights each week for the dining clientele.

We had landed on our feet.

Just across the street from our house was a giant supermarket. Acquainting myself with this American institution, I prowled the aisles, gaping in awe at the acres of cereals, washing powders, and pet foods. Growing up in Chesterfield, I was often grateful for a dinner of turnips and tea. In the States, one had the choice of twenty types of bread, dozens of soups, and at least fifty different brands of dog and cat food. I was stunned by the twenty-four-hour-a-day flaunting of the staples of life in twelve-foot high neon letters. There was more of everything in the States, and it was easier to get.

I was seduced. I'd never had it so good.

Ray was nothing if not a realist. After a week of rave reviews, he discussed the possibility of extending our engagement. By agreeing to extend our stay, he would have our services for what to him must have seemed a pittance. We shook hands on it, and for the first time in years we had a permanent gig paying real money on a regular basis.

Ray was a personable, highly literate, utterly irresponsible rogue. I took an immediate liking to him. It seemed that whenever Ruth and I came by, it was time to celebrate. He was always saving us his best filet mignon, or ordering his chef to prepare shrimp scampi just for us. It was always the best bottle of wine, or a glass of his oldest cognac.

He was that way with everyone. He was a true host, an innkeeper with genius, generous to everyone.

Our stay at the tavern lasted nearly a year. By that time we were well fed and well rested, with egos stroked and wallets comfortable. Perhaps best of all, we had devoted unbroken months to our art. Immediately after our arrival, we set up a studio in one of the large unused bedrooms of our house. Ruth sculpted, painted, and drew. I focused on painting and drawing, and achieved again the flowing looseness of creativity that I had not enjoyed since art school and the brief period of intense creativity during my first stay in Ramatuelle.

Spring and summer afforded us days in sunshine. We scoured the surrounding area, setting up canvases in and outside the city. Connecticut offered cityscapes, woods, lakes, and waterfalls within a short drive. We began going to Cape Cod when we could get away. The coast there was made for artists, and we began dreaming of buying a house in the area when we could manage.

But music continued to pay the bills, and solvency is among the finest of art forms. We felt that we had moved to a new level of expertise, both in performing and creating original material. We had come a long way from the streets of St. Tropez. Ruth's voice was stronger and more mature than ever. She was exploring new vocal dimensions. We had written a number of original songs and had considerable expertise now in stagework and presentation.

Boston was the Mecca of folk music in that era. To move to the next level, Boston is where we needed to be. Taking leave of Ray's generosity for a time, we found a suitably dilapidated basement apartment in Somerville and set about the task of finding gigs.

The year 1969 was a highpoint for the Boston music scene. Local musicians were making it big. James Taylor and his entire family, including the dog it seemed, were making records and selling millions. Things were bubbling. But not for Ruth and Kerry. We felt that we were missing the boat. Being passed over. History was repeating itself. We were beating the bushes for work. The bushes were winning.

The high spot of our Boston days was singing for a week at the Unicorn as the opening act for Tom Rush. We were certain that this engagement would springboard us into exposure with other clubs. But the pickings remained meager, and we were obliged to take tedious day jobs to put bread on the table and pay the rent.

That in itself was depressing. We kept a brave front, reassuring each other, but deep down we felt we had failed. Every day we waited, hoping for the phone call that would herald the start of a new musical ascension. We had the goods. We knew our stuff. We were good. What was taking so long? After months of this charade, one's energy starts to dip. Doubt creeps in, and it becomes increasingly difficult to remain positive. The spirit erodes and everything assembles towards an inevitable downward spiral.

A writer who worked for the local newspaper lived in an apartment above us. We knew him fairly well, and he had written a nice piece on us. One evening when we were having drinks, he told us that he was planning to go into the music business as a manager and might be interested in representing us. He had one other musician that he was considering and wanted to make a decision within the week whether to represent him or us. He outlined his plans and then asked a pointed question. "How badly do you want to become stars?"

After three years of paddling upstream, we had developed what to him must have seemed a somewhat cynical attitude. Our response was jumbled and tinged with bitterness. I'm sure we gave the impression of ambivalence. Truth is, we had run out of gas. By the end of the week he had decided to go with his other choice. That choice was Bruce Springsteen. The manager's name, John Landau.

44

Mary Wana

During the final evening of our week's engagement at the Unicorn, we were presented with a couple of joints as a farewell present. We'd shared a furtive smoke once or twice aboard yachts or in private parties in St. Tropez, but we had contented ourselves with the more traditional forms of intoxication: beer and wine with the odd cognac when things were flush.

We were advised that these joints were especially potent, and that we should have no pressing engagements when indulging. Next afternoon, invigorated by our week's success, we decided to celebrate. We invited our friend Didi, who lived on the fourth floor of our building, to share our present. Safe in our basement flat, we felt that the time was right for some fun and relaxation.

The joints took effect almost immediately. We drifted into the haze. Everything became amusingly absurd. We gave ourselves over, giggling and chortling with abandon. The music was swimming, the Turkish delight astonishing, the mind awash with visions. I was bathed in a glow of well-being, with no desire to do anything more demanding than close my eyes and float in the music.

A sudden loud banging at the door rocked the entire apartment. The noise was deafening, terrifying. Was it the police?

The FBI? The narcotics squad?

I went rigid. Obviously, I had to answer the door. Yes, that was required. I had to rise, walk over, reach down, turn the knob, and open the door.

No problem normally. But from my vantage point on the sofa, this seemed impossibly far away.

Whoever was on the outside would be wondering what was taking so long. With superhuman effort, I stood fully erect. I was at least two feet taller than when I had sat down. I managed to find my way to the door and opened it.

There stood the landlord. Rent day.

I gazed at him for an eternity, my mouth full of cotton and my lips numb. With a great effort and in slow, very slow motion, I orchestrated a sweeping two-handed bow, bidding him enter.

The landlord strode into the kitchen. Thankfully, Ruth and Didi were safe in the lounge, well out of earshot. The landlord stared at me, and I at him. I was trying to remain calm. I mustn't for one instant behave in any way that would be suspicious.

Conversation. That's what the situation called for.

"Would you like to try some of this yogurt and wheat germ?" I asked, flooding him with a massive smile.

"Thank you very much, just the check. I have to be on my way."

That's what it was, the rent check. Of course. Makes sense. But this was going to be difficult.

I found the checkbook. I fumbled through the pages and unscrewed the top from the enormous fountain pen. Writing the check was quite easy, but the nib made a deafening sound as it scratched across the paper.

"Sorry about the noise," I said.

He gave me a questioning look. I tore off the check and handed it to him.

"Enjoy the yogurt." He looked at me again quite strangely and left.

I rejoined the ladies in the smoking compartment and took several large hits from the joint. Now maybe I could settle down to some relaxation.

A few minutes later, we were rocked again by thunderous banging on the door. Lightning had struck twice.

I embarked on the same hazardous journey across the room

to the door. I didn't much care this time who was on the other side. My main concern was to maintain an appearance of decorum. I turned the door knob and pulled. Standing before me was a full grown priest, dog collar and all.

I panicked. I needed to be careful here. It could be a religious trap. When in doubt, give 'em a smile. I did an ear to ear.

"Atheist," I said, starting to close the door.

"Are you Kerry?" Hearing my name, I froze.

"Are you collecting?" I was losing control of the situation.

"I'm a friend of Didi's. They told me she was down here."

I felt considerably relieved, but what on earth was Didi doing inviting a priest to our unsavory celebration?

He made his way into the lounge, and Didi made an official introduction. She assured us that her friend was a very liberal priest, and that we shouldn't feel at all awkward.

I retired to the kitchen to reflect on this surreal turn of events. I decided that I should continue to play it safe. Every effort should be made to give an impression of pristine sobriety.

Tea. That would do the trick. What could be more proper and conservative? And maybe a cookie or two.

I set about the unbelievably complex task of assembling the pots, cups, bowls, spoons, trays, plates, and other paraphernalia. No wonder the Chinese make an art of this. Boiling the water was a terrible drain on my flagging stamina, but at last I had gathered all the necessary ingredients.

I carried the twelve-foot wide tray into the next room and placed it on the table. My smile had become such a permanent fixture that my ears were getting tired. I was close to exhaustion from the efforts I had made to keep up a normal appearance. One last effort would accomplish it, I thought.

"Tea, Vicar?" I poured and most of it hit the cup. The milk missed completely. I couldn't find the sugar bowl.

One last gesture. Some remark to certify normalcy.

Clutching my cup, I smiled and fixed the priest in my sights. I took a sip, considering what I should say, and came up with the perfect remark to assure him all was well.

"You have no idea how large my nose feels," I said, tea dribbling down my chin.

45
Ruth & Kerry Finale

W e'd had a tremendous run of it. We had entertained princes and royalty, along with thousands of other more common folks in need of a lighthearted evening. We had sung in concert halls, cabarets, cafés, winecellers, and recording studios. We had entertained rich and poor on yachts and rooftops, and had reached the masses through television, radio, and film. We had traveled the length and breadth of Europe and much of the Eastern seaboard of the United States.

For the most part it had been a blast.

Now it was getting stale.

We were not, it seemed, destined to reach the plateau we had longed for. We were both tired. We needed a rest.

A year or so earlier, during one of our concerts in Germany, Ruth had left the stage to undergo an emergency appendectomy. The operation was serious. She'd been fighting the pain all day, completely caught in the feeling that the show must go on.

She resumed work far too soon. She was a fighter and refused even to consider resting as she should. Within two weeks of the operation, she was in front of an audience. She should have taken at least a month. Of course, we were facing the ever-present reality of "no sing, no money." She felt she had to keep working to keep us afloat. Over the ensuing months, the ex-

hausting operation caught up to her and wore her down.
Sitting in our basement Boston apartment, the gigs beginning again to run thin, we agreed that it was time to hang up
the guitars for a spell and take solid day jobs.
Working nine to five was a poor substitute for the glamour
and freedom of our life as a singing duo. Our relationship became more difficult, and we found ourselves talking about sepa-
rating. This was a confusing, demoralizing time. It seemed to
us that we were failing on two fronts: not only were we ending
our music careers, we were ending a marriage.
Ruth moved upstairs with Didi. We told each other that
the separation was temporary. This made things seem less final and less painful.
We both knew it was the end.
Ruth and I had been together for the better part of five years.
We had progressed through fat and lean, along a road of extreme ups and downs. But always we enjoyed the security of a
close bond and a very special kind of friendship. Us against
them! We'll be at the top someday!
And what could be more delightful, really?
We probably had spent more time together than most
couples over a lifetime of marriage. Not only had we been husband and wife, we had been partners and fellow travelers on
the road to fortune. Ruth had been my confidante; someone I
trusted totally. This made for a very close, if somewhat con-
stricted relationship.
We both tried hard to make a go of the married part, without success. Ruth finally found the courage to confront this head
on. It wasn't easy, but I knew the wisdom of her decision.

46

Boston Common

I was astounded at the emptiness Ruth's departure left. Eve nings were very quiet. Weekends somber and lonely. I found myself staying out later than I wanted and leaving the apartment early in the morning.

Not feeling at all like painting, I did my best to find singing gigs. Eventually, I decided that my best bet would be to produce a demo album from the collection of songs that I had composed. Such an album could be used as a calling card to be sent to recording companies.

By then I had assembled twenty or more songs that were ready for the hit parade. All it takes is one hit and you're made, right? I must say that in my rather reduced circumstances, it was hard to see how this would happen. Optimism makes reality superfluous.

However, a well-heeled friend from Paris offered to put up funds to make the demo at a local studio. He believed in my songs, and the studio people liked the music enough to work for cut rates with a percentage of future profits. We were looking forward to producing an album that would knock the pop world on its arse.

We selected fourteen original songs from my repertoire and began the laborious task of arranging them for recording. We spent weeks rehearsing and refining the numbers, until we were sure they were note-for-note perfect.

The great day arrived. In anticipation, I brought with me to the studio a few six packs of beer and a bottle of scotch. Everyone promptly got drunk in celebration, and by midafternoon we still hadn't started the first take. We decided to leave it and start fresh in the morning.

I spent the rest of the evening worrying. It had not been a good start. We didn't have the normal constraints of astronomical studio fees, but there was a limit to my friend's generosity. Having had considerable studio experience, I was confident that we could complete the album in a matter of days.

It took the best part of a month.

Ultimately, we were obliged to leave certain of the final tracks without a complete mix. We had run out of time and cash. The album was, however, a strong collection. It was more than adequate to send to the major recording companies to demonstrate my potential.

Despite the enormous strain of having to co-produce my own album, the songs sounded polished. The underlying message to recording companies was clear and straightforward: if we achieved this quality on a shoestring, just imagine what your top-of-the-line engineers could do with the material in a full-production facility.

I sent forty or more albums with cover letters to every recording company of note in the U.S. and London. As we awaited return calls, I planned how I would spend the first million.

Weeks went by without a single call. I received no communication whatsoever, not even a thank you or a drop dead. I couldn't believe it. Surely someone in the higher echelons of the recording industry had to have enough of a musical ear to recognize genius when it's placed on their desk.

I realize now that I was being sublimely naive. More than likely, no one of significance ever heard my demo albums. Things don't work that way. One has to know someone who knows someone. One has to be versed in the subtle arts of skullduggery and arse licking. I was following the path of blind faith and complete naivete. Many, more talented than I, have fallen into the same trap.

Enthusiasm is no substitute for a solid manager. I spent a

month or so feeling depressed and licking my wounds, then went back to washing dishes and playing at the odd local bar and coffee house.

One afternoon, I received a call from the mayor's office in Boston. The person in charge of summer events offered me a gig playing a forty-minute set at a function on the Boston Common. Scheduled for the ninth of June, the event was to be called "June Art In the Park."

The gig paid sixty dollars.

"I'd love to do it," I told him. "But I'll have to pay my bass and electric guitar twenty each. Couldn't you make it a hundred?"

"Sorry, Kerry. That's the budget. You don't have to take it, but it might do you some good, open a few doors. What do you say?"

I began to recognise the verbiage that usually accompanied this kind of bloodsucking offer.

"I'll take it. Thanks a lot." What cheek. Twenty bucks after expenses, really.

My friends, who had worked with me on my demo album, agreed to help. We decided just to meet at the gig. We had no incentive to rehearse. We knew the songs backwards, and anyway, for twenty bucks each . . . .

A few other friends suggested that since it was an Art Show, why not take a few of my paintings and hang them up for sale? I agreed, with no great enthusiasm. It seemed like a waste of time, but what the hell? Nothing ventured, nothing gained. I'd kept my hand in with oils and acrylics. I had ten or fifteen works I was rather proud of just hanging on the walls doing the old pocketbook no good.

My friends were enthusiastic. Bless them all. I helped them pack a dozen or so pieces into the back of an old van and thought nothing more about it.

June the ninth was blistering and oppressively humid. In the mid-nineties and pushing upward.

When we arrived at the venue, the organiser told us the show would start at midday. We were to play on a stage with no canopy. The sun beat straight down and seemed to be melting everything by ten o'clock. Mad dogs, I thought!

The sound system was comprised of one mike and a single small amplifier that would have to accommodate both the bass and lead guitars. This meant that I could either mike my voice or my guitar, but not both-unless I contorted my body in a manner yet unknown to man.

There were no monitors, so we would have no idea what we sounded like. I pointed this out to the emcee.

"Big deal. Don't waste my time. Why worry, anyway?"

For twenty bucks, I got the message. When at twelve noon we began and were unable to hear each other, we didn't worry. When perspiration was running down our fretboards in rivers, we didn't worry. When the bass player popped a string, we didn't worry. When no one strolling the common gave us so much as a passing glance, let alone applause, we didn't worry.

And when I finally turned to my friends and said, "Screw this for a game of silly buggers let's pack it in now," we didn't worry.

When the emcee came up to us as were packing and remarked that we were supposed to play for forty minutes, and when I told him to stick his gig where the sun doesn't shine, we didn't worry.

They had made the mistake of paying us in cash before we went on, so we certainly weren't about to worry.

My friends went off to find a cool bar, and I sought out my mates staffing my painting exhibit. They had set up shop by a fence at the side of the common.

Their faces lit up when they saw me coming. One of the girls ran toward me and grabbed my arm. She pulled me toward the tidy little booth she and a few of her friends had assembled.

During my less-than-scintillating debacle on stage, they had sold four hundred dollars worth of paintings.

It was a blessed epiphany.

I had sweated my arse off for twenty dollars, while they had made twenty times as much sitting around chatting with people about painting.

By the end of the day, we had taken in several hundred dollars more and were heading home with rent and food money for a month.

We threw a huge party to celebrate. Wine and good feelings flowed in all directions. We agreed that life again was indeed very rosy.

Late that evening, as the last of our friends left, I took down my oil painting palette, which had been serving as a tasteful accent on the bedroom wall. I replaced it with my Guild F50 guitar.

The fog had cleared. The signpost was easy to read.

Music was put on the back burner, painting brought to the fore.

47

Weekend Art Shows

I painted at a feverish pace. I was tremendously motivated to make up for the years I had spent on futile musical efforts. I set myself a demanding schedule, often painting until dawn. Almost out of thin air I had been given the chance to do something that would generate an income. I felt great promise. After all, I had an education in this field. Four solid years of it. Hardly a week had gone by since my paper-delivery days that I hadn't done a drawing or painting of some sort.

I scanned local newspapers and located innumerable outdoor shows each weekend throughout the greater Boston area. Afraid to get paint on the carpet of my apartment, I rigged up lights in the basement of the building and set up my studio next to the water heater, where the local chapter of spiders had their nightly meetings. I felt a little like Gulliver, but grew accustomed to working while tangled in their webs.

In my strained financial condition, painting materials were expensive. Evenings I spent foraging for materials to use in place of canvas. Construction sites and abandoned lots invariably produced wood or masonite panels on which I could paint. Brushes were a problem. Simply put, I didn't have any and couldn't afford to buy them. I improvised with my fingers, various kitchen utensils, and bits of cloth.

The results of that period were somewhat monochromatic. I was using mostly house paint with the odd dash of Winsor & Newton from a few crusty tubes.

Within two weeks I had assembled about twenty pieces and was ready to launch my career at a show on the Cambridge Common. I arrived early to set up my display, which consisted of two wooden doors slung between a couple of uprights. I hung the paintings on hooks. I'd managed to put together a few lattice frames, which gave a little finish to the works.

There must have been a hundred or more artists and craftspeople at the show. The variety of artwork was truly awesome. I was heartened that much of the work was by people who couldn't have painted their way out of a public urinal. They had no business foisting their inarticulate and amateur daubings on the unsuspecting public.

Surely this would give me an edge. At least my work had some evidence of acumen. Then, too, strolling through the exhibits, I couldn't help feel that my work had some individual style. I felt strongly that my art education and years of awareness of painting and drawing had given me a solid foundation.

I learned a very valuable lesson during this first show: "No one ever went broke underestimating the public taste."

The lady next to me was selling "Original Oil Paintings by Mary Jo." This homey epithet was emblazoned on a large wooden sign above her very elaborate display. Her Sunday hobby paintings measured about five inches by seven. All were in gaudy gold rococo frames bought at the local supermarket. For practical purposes, all her paintings were identical. Each consisted of a wispy rendering of vase and table, blobs of colour straight from the tube representing flowers, and an attempt at foliage using a spastic brushstroke or two.

They wouldn't have sold any faster if she had been giving them away.

She must have started with a hundred or more pieces of this garbage hanging in her booth. As the day progressed, I watched her return repeatedly to her stationwagon for replacements.

Mary Jo was her own salesperson. She maintained an incessant babble of aggressive good humour as she dispensed her wares to clamoring housewives. The general accolade was that her paintings were "cute."

By the end of the day, she must have pocketed the best part of two thousand dollars. She was still going at it as I packed to leave. She may still be there, for all I know.

As I did more shows, it became evident that appreciation of such work was the rule rather than the exception. It rankled, but I refused to stoop to a lower level. I tried with every painting to capture a particular feeling or memory. I simply could not paint unless I felt the urge to express something in the work.

Fortunately, there was an audience for such ambitions. Several times during every show an individual or couple browsing through the booths suddenly would become interested in one of my pieces. They would comment on the colouration or overall design, on the emotional impact, on the achievement of purpose.

I lived for such moments.

Sales improved. After a particularly good show in Rhode Island, I could afford to buy a few real canvases and professional supplies. I was still in the basement with the spiders, but things were looking up.

That fall, I was introduced to a lady who organised mall exhibits during the winter. I was relieved to be accepted by her because the summer outdoor shows were getting thin on the ground.

Ms. Mallmadame was a good-looking woman — a quality camouflaged by her severe disposition and tyrannical temper. She demanded complete control and utter obedience from all who sailed with her. Inflexible insistence on sticking to the rules bordered on the psychotic. Woebetide any unfortunate exhibitor who was not "set up" at the scheduled place and time.

My first encounter with the Mall Show Circuit was in Burlington, a small town just outside Boston. Burlington was a busy shopping spot for suburban families. Other participants assured me that our time there would be lucrative.

I arrived the night before to set up my display, which now included a large collection of recent works in full colour, each with stunning frame. Assigned a spot outside Woolworth on the mall, I was fully prepared for the windfall that would accrue as the four days of the show progressed.

Woolworth's marketing and display personnel had decided to capitalize on the aesthetic atmosphere created by the art exhibit. They had decked out their windows with the best in prints on cardboard. These ranged from paintings of clowns with glistening tears running down their cheeks (the ultimate futility of life, after all) to ducks flying for their lives as hunters blasted the living crap out of them with shotguns. There was a selection of little girls collecting flowers and, of course, innumerable cat and puppy sketches.

Simply put, the windows were ablaze with all that is awful.

The artist next to me arrived and set up his easel. Facing Woolworth's window, he proceeded to execute several outstandingly inept copies of the prints on display. I watched in absolute disbelief as he slipped them, still wet, into frames and hung them on his rack for sale.

This performance continued throughout the four days. He sold every one he painted, finishing the show with pockets bulging.

I sold one small piece. This barely covered the show fee, transportation, and food. On the way home, I allowed myself a few of the dollars for several well-deserved and much-needed cognacs.

It was becoming clear to me that the term "art" had a totally different connotation on the American side of the Atlantic. My art professors must have been turning in their graves. I must say that I had feelings of betrayal for participating in such junkets. Still, I needed to make a living. I was gratified that a few good artists toured with the circuit, making life bearable.

I buckled down and resumed production, still not compromising my work. With each brushstroke I tried to capture the essence of my subject. Ultimately, this paid off. After a successful exhibit in the affluent Washington D.C. area, I drove home with over a thousand dollars in my pocket.

My course for the next ten years was set.

48

Couch Art

To my knowledge, there are still art tours travelling throughout the United States, and still artists who travel with them. The great shopping public spends enormous amounts of money on "original oil paintings," ceramics, decorated coat hangers, posters, brass leaf clusters, dolls, and almost anything that is produced in Korea and can sell for less than ten dollars as an original craft.

I knew artists who sold tinted photographs as original paintings and got away with it for years. Mass-produced planters were offered as expensive, one-of-a-kind china. When you stop to think about it, the public is taken for a hell of a ride daily. That is a given in almost every facet of our perverse economic structure. One rarely gets what one pays for.

I estimate that the public purchased close to $500,000 of "art" during one year of the tour in which I traveled. In current dollars, the $500,000 certainly would be worth $2 million or more. At least a dozen such tours circled the country regularly. Two million dollars multiplied by twelve is an impressive figure, considering that much of that money was spent on worthless junk dressed up as art, or at least as craft. I venture that most of the purchases have by now been relegated to an attic, tag sale, or a local thrift shop.

Regardless, I continued trying to maintain a reasonable

standard in the work I produced. The quality fluctuated, as is the rule for all artistic activity. Original oils and acrylics are not synthetic items stamped out on enormous presses in Taiwan. Each is unique, the product of a human being's emotional and mental makeup, which change hourly.

I have known quite a few "artists" who make a satisfactory living selling work for which a first-year student at the art school I attended would be severely censured, if not expelled. There's a lot of bad art out there, and a very large market for it.

Why?

Consider this scenario. Most people receive art education only during elementary school. This usually comprises a smattering of art history, fingerpainting, the making of plastercine sculpture, and maybe some simple craftwork-like leather carving or potato cutting.

Through middle school and high school, students are oriented entirely toward "practical" studies, such as English and math. High school students who take art classes are usually thought of as odd birds. The majority of Americans take no art classes whatsoever after the age of nine or ten.

Once in college, students study in their chosen fields. They emerge a few years later as fully qualified accountants, doctors, lawyers, businesspeople, or whatever. They then enter the work force. Several decades of hard labor follow, and middle age suddenly arrives. A person has a spouse, one and a half houses, one and a half cars, and one and a half kids. Quite often, a person also has one and a half ulcers and high cholesterol.

The family holds a meeting. It decides that to keep up with the Joneses, to be *au courant* and in step with the times, the living room needs a painting over the couch.

It is by that time probably twenty-five or thirty years since husband and wife have had any contact with art. They lack the necessary artistic faculty to purchase a painting with confidence or enjoyment. Any piece of work requiring more than a minimal level of art appreciation will be frightening. Our couple will be out of their depth looking at serious art. They will be sailing in dangerous, uncharted waters.

So they end up with something that matches the couch and

fits with the decor. What chance would a developing and still unknown Matisse, Van Gogh, or Cezanne have in this situation?

Sadly, we have to acknowledge that our "artist" stands a better chance of reaching this mainstream market by daubbing white paint over a gray canvas, popping in a few ducks, stippling on a couple of pine trees, and spattering snow over the whole thing.

This is what we see in art lessons on TV. It's what we see for the most part in mall shows. And, unfortunately, it's what we see over most couches.

49
Motor Homes

One prerequisite for those wishing to join the travelling art circus was the capacity to be completely self-sufficient. The organisers considered that since they went to the trouble of locating a spot in a mall to display our goods, the rest should be up to us. We artists had to fend for ourselves.

Shows usually ran from Wednesday to Sunday, during which time we were occupied day and night by sitting at our booths, selling our wares and during the odd moment working on new pieces. Monday was spent getting one's life back in order-washing clothes, restocking the liquor cabinet, etc. Tuesday was spent on the road.

At times, we had to drive hundreds of miles between shows. This meant breaking down the display (including lighting, tables, chairs, panels, easels, and braces) and loading it into a vehicle. Next came loading one's paintings (best not to forget those little items), then driving hell-for-leather to arrive in time to set up at the next venue.

Artists on tour frequently made overnight marathon drives and stayed at one seedy motel after another. To avoid the latter, many of the regulars opted for living in either a motor home or a travel trailer.

I went through a very checkered selection of mobile living

quarters. When I first joined the tour, I had a small display and small paintings. I could fit everything into a Dodge van. This vehicle/home-away-from-home had all the charms of a crack cocaine pad in the Bronx; a mattress to sleep on, a little gas ring for boiling water, and a hole in the floor to pee out of.

I was, at least, totally self-contained. I could sleep with satisfaction in the parking lot of a McDonalds thinking of the money I was saving on motel bills. More often than not, the Golden Arches also provided breakfast and a clean toilet with reasonably hot water. If I took care of business quickly, I could usually manage a strip wash and shave before the manager realized what was going on and rousted me out.

As my income increased, so did the size of my display. I was finally obliged to buy a travel trailer. I started with a small used sixteen-foot Midas. It had a real bathroom (no holes in the floor), a refrigerator, air conditioner, stove, and large comfy bed.

I had some fine times in my Midas, but it finally gave up the ghost. I replaced it with a much larger, much fancier model that had a revolutionary new feature: insulation. The manufacturer guaranteed that you could camp at the North Pole and be comfortable.

I was delighted. It was cooler in summer and warmer in winter. But there's always a trade-off. The insulation made the trailer a lot heavier. To haul it, I had to get a van with a larger engine. The gas pumps loved to see me coming. I was getting about eleven miles to the gallon even on the open road.

Next, I tried a motor home proper. It was a monstrous "top of the line," "state of the art," "latest in everything" thirty-four foot Apollo. It had a microwave, built-in vacuum, colour TV, and ice maker. Fully loaded with all my gear, display and paintings, it must have weighed in at ten tons or more. The gas pumps weren't just glad to see me coming. They phoned and asked when I would be arriving.

I ended up, as all dedicated campers do, with the ultimate luxury travel trailer — a "Tri Axle Avion." This truly majestic, aluminum, six-wheel travel trailer had absolutely everything that anyone could ever wish. It was light to pull, aerodynamic and very, very cushy inside. I had it right up to the end of my trailering days, and I never had the slightest doubt that I had spent my money wisely.

I gradually lost my liking for motor homes. They are cumbersome monstrosities, absolute gas guzzlers. On top of it all, when you park and then want to pop down the road for some milk or a bottle of plonk, you have to repack everything. It gets to be most tiresome at the end of a long drive.

I toured with art shows for the best part of ten years. Hardly ever did I make enough money to escape the tours' clutches. Expenses were exorbitant. I continually found myself in a position similar to what Ruth and I had experienced during our touring days in Germany: at the end of a tour, I had just enough money to start on the next.

It ran thin. But I honed my craft, becoming a better artist. I met many fine people (a few among them exceptional artists) and enjoyed a lifetime of experience crammed into a decade.

50

Bowler

B owler's massive shoulders made him look like a full back. He attacked life as though he were sacking it. He was a diabetic who consumed gallons of beer daily. His enormous intake of food and drink should have killed him, but somehow he stayed alive.

He told us that he had a wife in Oklahoma. We never knew whether that was true. He traveled with a parrot, a large piano, a charcoal grill, and an arsenal of firearms.

Bowler had been one of the founding members of the California chapter of Hell's Angels, but he had gone astray. He fell in with a bad lot and ended up an artist.

His brochure described his artistic beginnings. It maintained that whilst serving his country in Korea, his platoon had been wiped out on a sortie. Badly wounded and barely alive amidst fire and smoke and dead companions, Bowler sat propped up against the wall of a ruined chapel. A shaft of sunlight pierced the haze, lighting the far wall. He lifted his eyes and saw murals of angels with golden halos.

In his delirium, he was convinced that he had seen the hand of God. He vowed that if he survived, he would learn to paint using gold leaf, as in the mural, and devote the rest of his life to art.

One evening he told me the real story.

Late one night a decade or so before I met him, Bowler had

189

been leaving a diner somewhere in the Deep South. A painting on the wall stopped him in his tracks. (If the painting hadn't, the sheer quantity of beer he had consumed would have.) He was entranced. He bought it from the owner, looked up the artist, learned how to apply gold leaf, and started a new career.

Twenty-four karat gold leaf is expensive, but aluminum foil looks virtually the same to the untrained eye and is far less fragile. Bowler went to work with a vengeance. He learned to paint a tree, a mountain, a wave. Enclosing them with just a touch of aluminum foil yielded an "expensive," "original," "inspired-by-a-vision" gold leaf painting. That was enough to launch his art crusade on the unsuspecting world.

Bowler had an imposing presence and was an unyielding salesman. I recall watching him in action one time when an irate customer stormed into Bowler's booth, carrying the painting his wife had bought the day before.

"We hung it up last night. This morning one of the trees had fallen off."

A problem? Not for Bowler. Not only did he calm the irate husband, he sold him two more paintings. "It fell off because the work is so delicate. I sold it for less than the cost of my materials. Takes me months for each piece. Like this little beauty here. . . ."

Bowler was an enigma. He was generous to a fault but not past screwing you just for the exercise. He was angry and violent but capable of childlike gentleness that could melt the hardest heart. He was vulgar but disarmingly courteous. He was rough and rude, yet capable of great warmth.

He was the unspoken leader of our group. Every night after the mall closed, we gathered outside his trailer. Out came the parrot, the charcoal grill, the chicken, and the beer. Belching and farting as though his life depended on it, he would entertain us with ribald stories, describing the glory days of biking, drinking, and leching. Inevitably, he finished by playing his piano. He played very badly but with tremendous gusto.

I became one of his close circle because of my guitar playing. It added musical dimension to his nightly gathering. I'm sure that there are neighborhoods around the country that still remember one or another of our 3:00 a.m. renditions of "The

House of the Rising Sun".

He became something of a legend among art-tour aficionados. Stories of his outrageous behavior were elaborated and stretched to the point of religious adoration. They were added to and embellished until bearing no resemblance to the actual events.

Each had a grain of truth, however. After all, most good folk tales and almost all religious organisations have evolved via the same system: misinterpretation and ultimate glorification.

One of Bowler's finest moments stands firmly in my recollection. The organisers of the show advised us that big wigs from the mall's head office would visit us at 10 a.m. the following morning. We were expected to have our areas spruced up and to wear appropriate clothing.

I was set up next to Bowler, but by ten there was no sign of him. I knew he had been visiting a house of ill repute the previous evening, so I slipped into his booth and turned on the lights.

The owners and our two organisers began winding their way through the booths. Their patronizing tones floated toward me as the various exhibitors were presented for inspection. I was beginning to worry. Normally, we could cover for Bowler, but this was going to be tricky.

With all the pomposity of a royal command performance, the group walked into my booth. I was presented.

"Lovely work."

"Delightful."

"Very nice."

The group edged their way into Bowler's booth.

"I'm so sorry. The artist seems to be indisposed at the moment," cooed our director.

Just then, with a whooshing sound from the tall plants next to the booth, Bowler emerged as though he had been hacking his way through the Malay jungle. He was in total disarray. A few leaves were caught in his matted, uncombed hair. His eyes were bloodshot, his shirt ripped and stained. He smelled like a brewery.

As he staggered toward the astonished group, his trousers slipped halfway down his thighs.

"Morning — indisposed — just taking a piss in the jungle-
oh, nice lady — let me take you to my trailer — great knockers
— er, got a light — how many paintings do you want? — cash
only — "

His trousers fell fully to the floor and he collapsed into the
shrubbery. The terrified group moved on to the security of the
wildlife artist in the next booth.

You might think that Bowler would be removed from the
tour after that. Hardly. He was a moneymaker.

"Just tell Hallam to cover for you next time," the director
told him afterward. "At least he can keep his pants up in public."

51

Sasha

Janora Karoly Ischanorinovitch was a hell of a mouthful. Wisely, he had adopted the nickname "Sasha." It made conversation with him a lot easier.

Sasha was one of the most talented artists I have ever met. He was capable of stunning depth in his work. His intense paintings were etched with profound statements of the human condition. He enjoyed impeccable draughtsmanship and consummate artistic skill.

As a person, he was a complete lout. He was rude, arrogant, and misanthropic. He should not have been allowed anywhere near the art-show circuit. His work was far too artistic to enjoy regular success. Occasionally, however, someone came along and bought a few pieces, thus condemning him to continue.

Born in Croatia, Sasha was reluctant to talk about his early life. I managed to glean some information from him one night after prolonged consumption of good red wine. He was born of nobility. In fact, he was a count — and still would have been if he'd had a country. Well educated, he had been destined for a life of finery until the Nazis marched in and changed his world forever.

The Germans immediately conscripted him as a soldier. His father was shot. His sister and mother were taken hostage to ensure that Sasha would behave. Having little alternative, he pretended to embrace the Nazi regime with great verve. So fine was his act that they promoted him a few times and gave him special posts. This saved his mother and sister from certain extermination in a concentration camp.

Sasha's scope of activity went far beyond what the Third Reich knew of him. Over the next five years, Sasha quietly organised the escape of hundreds of prisoners of war: Americans, Englishmen, and Jews of all nationalities. His activities were never acknowledged since that would have meant certain death. But there are hundreds or even thousands of people alive today because of his bravery.

At the end of the war, he studied art in Rome. England had refused to let him into the country, thank you very much. Becoming disillusioned with the academic life, penniless and unable to settle down, he moved to Paris and sold his paintings on the street in Monmartre.

That was probably the first time since his childhood that he had enjoyed a shred of security and peace. But after a time, his paintings stopped selling. There were few buyers for his brooding, abstract canvases. His income fell to zero, then to less than zero. Again he found himself rejected.

Using one of his many contacts, he moved to America. By that time he had become a bitter man. His complexity deepened and twisted. For some reason, after having saved the lives of so many, he became violently anti-Semitic, anti-American, anti-British, and anti-French. By the time I met him, he had become anti-everything.

He emerged a man at siege with himself. But his painting was unaffected. He continued to produce a dazzling collection of sensitive and powerfuly expressive abstracts. Occasionally I saw him attempt to paint a commercial piece (mountains, lakes, pines, etc.), but he did it without conviction. Inevitably he returned to his symbolism. Only that could soothe his demons.

A gypsy artist, he did his best to fit into a group with which he had nothing in common. His English was poor, as was his German and French. His anesthetic was red wine and cigarettes. After a few bottles, he mellowed, but few of his fellow artists could tolerate his fierce antisocial posture.

Sasha died a couple of years ago. He wasn't that old, 65 maybe. I found out too late to attend the funeral. He was a friend, though I don't really know why. I hated his despotic bigotry, his anti-Semitic slurs, his constant depredation of every race, color, and creed.

Somewhere inside Sasha was a person eager to be understood and appreciated. It was never given a chance to come out, except in his paintings. God knows where they are now.

One evening after closing the show, we were all sitting around passing time. I was playing guitar and leading the group in a few old favorites: "Blowin' in the Wind", "John Henry", "Michael Row Your Boat".

Everyone was a little drunk, the mood boisterous and jocular. I began strumming a song I'd heard years before. I didn't know its name. Didn't know where it came from.

Imperceptibly at first, a deep bass voice insinuated itself upon us. It grew louder, insistent. I covered the guitar strings. Talk subsided.

The bass voice grew stronger, singing in an unfamiliar, vastly foreign tongue. Goosebumps stood up on my arms. The voice weaved in and out of the parked trailers, around the dim figures huddled by the barbecue, then soared and spiralled upward over the shopping mall.

Sasha finished the song with eyes closed. His head was erect, his arms folded in his lap. Tears rolled down his cheeks.

"It is a song of my childhood," he said. "It's about love."

Quietly he rose and stumbled toward his trailer. We were left with the remains of a Croatian lullaby.

52

Pete and Chance

Pete and Chance, two artists on the tour, were buddies. Standing together, they looked like 1940 Hollywood. They personified middle-aged sex appeal. Both were stunningly handsome with close-cut graying hair, steely blue eyes, square jaws, trimmed mustaches, and rugged features. Both were about six feet tall, lithe and athletic, with easy walks and soft lilting voices.

Chance should have been born sixty years earlier. He came from Montana and was a cowboy through and through. I never saw him without his Stetson, jeans, denim jacket, and high-heeled boots. He dreamed of owning a ranch. All he really wanted out of life was to round up the dogies and sing cowboy songs to the clear skies of his beloved Montana. His paintings of the Old West reflected this, and sold well to a certain clientele.

Pete, on the other hand, was from Washington, D.C. A reformed advertising executive, he had seen the light and taken to the road, hawking his pastel renditions of western movie stars. His booth was studded with paintings of John Wayne, Gary Cooper, Roy Rogers, etc.

Chance, being a real cowboy born and bred, became Pete's idol. Pete copied Chance's style and mannerisms to the last detail. He would have given anything to be like Chance, but try as he might, a chunk of ad man always seemed to remain inside him. Pete's surface was Western, his core D.C.

Chance had a hunting dog named — what else — Blue. The dog was Chance's faithful companion, so naturally Pete had to get a dog, too. He bought a French hunting dog, which from the start didn't seem to acknowledge the responsibility of being "Western."

Pete named it "Fluffy."

Almost immediately, the dog became a problem. It chewed on everything in sight. It left droppings everywhere willy-nilly, whined constantly, and was utterly unmanageable. It had to be kept on a leash because when let loose, it would run in a blind frenzy until exhausted. Call as Pete might, it would not return.

Chance confided to Pete one day. "Dogs are like folk. Some are born without all the right tackle. You're gonna have problems with that hound, I can tell you."

Sure enough, there were problems. Pete had to keep the dog in a large cage. He let it out only when absolutely necessary.

One night when the tour was camping in a North Carolina state park, Chance took Blue out for some exercise. Every few minutes Chance would whistle. Blue would instantly halt and remain motionless, awaiting the next command.

Blue was a wonderful example of canine intelligence. He never missed a signal. Seeing this, Pete decided to see how Fluffy would do. Pete unlocked the cage and led the crazed, panting dog into the field, where he released its chain. Fluffy took off running at tremendous speed in a wide circle around the outer perimeter of the park. Pete whistled, shouted, screamed, pleaded and implored, but Fluffy continued the frantic race.

An hour later, the exhausted dog was put back in its cage. Pete sat for the rest of the evening in a state of total depression.

On another occasion, the tour was staying in a campground by the ocean in northern Florida. After unhitching trailers and connecting water and electricity, Chance took Blue down a little stairway leading to the beach.

Pete thought he'd let Fluffy out of the cage and go with

them. He carefully attached the leash, but as soon as the cage door was open, Fluffy bounded over Pete's head and started dragging him toward the high bluff overlooking the water. Without hesitating, Fluffy leaped over the bluff and hung by the leash as Pete tried to pull him up. Strangling, squealing, in full canine hysterics, Fluffy dangled for a full minute until Pete could slide the leash to the stairway. Once there, Pete dragged Fluffy to safety and flopped him on the sand.

Pete probably knew what was in store as he bent down to undo Fluffy's leash. The dog zipped off like a bullet. It was the fastest animal I have ever seen. It flew like a jet plane to the edge of the water, to the bluff, to Chance, to Blue, to me, back to the seaside, and then . . .

We lost sight of Fluffy at around three-quarters of a mile. The crazy zigzag pattern finally disappeared, never to show up again.

That evening, Chance took Pete and Blue for a beer at the local honky-tonk. When I ran into them, I sensed on both their parts sadness, and relief, at the loss of Fluffy.

The rest of us were delighted.

53
Irene

One of the more exotic speed bumps during my stint with the travelling art circus was Irene.

Late in the morning at a mall show in Clearwater, Florida, I was putting the finishing touches on a rather nice Mediterranean harbour. I wasn't too keen on working, but the show was slow, even for the retirement capital of America. With the dearth of customers, I felt obliged to increase my inventory. One could never have too many paintings.

I was trying my best to concentrate amid the ponderous procession of retirees who were spending their day in the air-conditioned luxury of the mall.

Being retired is a thankless task. You spend your life working like hell, raising the kids, saving the pennies so you can afford a little peace and contentment during the waning years of your life. You buy a condo for yourself and the wife and move to sunny Florida.

What awaits you? Shuffleboard and Friday afternoon bingo.

They promised you a golden reward for your lifelong dedication. What you get is Disney World and the Interstate.

It's not right. It's not fair. Someone should do something about it.

You find yourself sitting around bemoaning the state of

things and comparing symptoms and hoping to hell that you win the lottery so you can go back to Jersey, where at least they serve a decent matzo ball and you'd be able to see your grandchildren once in a while.

So you take the bus to the mall for early lunch at Morrison's Cafeteria. You follow this with a stroll to the end and back before catching the bus home.

This general state of affairs does not beget what you might call an encouraging atmosphere in which to sell paintings.

Anyway, there I was, dabbing away at my painting, fending off the usual deluge of questions.

"Do you do this for a living?"

"My friend paints. Beautiful flowers, so real. And cats, too. Do you think she could sell them?"

I was mixing the colours for a particularly stubborn passage in the reflection of one of the boats, when I had the strange feeling that I was being watched. Not the ordinary feeling you get when you're working in public. More insistent and disturbing.

I looked around but saw nothing unusual. I returned to my painting, but the feeling persisted. Turning again, I glanced upward. On the balcony above stood an absolutely gorgeous girl. She gazed down at me with an inquisitive look on her face.

I smiled. She smiled.

"It looks pretty good from up here!"

"Distance tends to blur the rough spots!" I was pleased with that one. Witty and casual. "Why don't you come down and take a closer look?"

"I'm working in the restaurant right now. Maybe later."

She left to seat an elderly couple.

I decided to take an early lunch and investigate the restaurant a little further. It proved a rewarding decision.

I had salad, wine, and a cup of coffee. They were served exclusively by the girl whose gaze had caused my consternation. She was definitely giving me her full attention.

Later that afternoon, when she finished work, she invited herself to my trailer for tea and a personal tour of my sketches. Two days (and nights) later, we emerged. She had not seen my sketches, but what she had showed me was infinitely more interesting and a good deal more personal.

Irene was half American Indian. The other half wasn't significant. She was dark, exotic, and desperately beautiful. In the right light, she was like one of Gaughin's Tahitian beauties: mysterious and brooding.

She loved her body and the pleasure it could give her. As far as she was concerned, life was dedicated to that single pursuit. Everything else, including me, was a means to that end. When the show pulled out five days later, she quit her job and joined me to experience firsthand the great travelling art circus.

What a delight for me. She was a gourmet cook, a natural salesperson, an enlivening companion, and a tremendous lover. We celebrated for three exhausting months all the way up the Eastern seaboard. One day during a show in Canada, however, she announced that she wanted to return to Florida. She would get a job and set up house so I could join her after the summer season.

I was a little taken aback, but secretly I was relieved at the possibility of some undisturbed rest. The feast had been thrilling, but Irene's galloping sexual appetite had worn me down. It stood in the way of really getting to know her. And I needed to get some paintings done.

She flew out of Toronto and two weeks later wrote to say that she had found a job in a health spa. She had bought a car and set up a comfy apartment. Was I planning to come to Florida soon?

I couldn't leave the tour at that moment. Too many promising venues remained. I called her and arranged to fly down for a visit when the good shows were completed.

When I could finally get away, she met me at the Tampa airport. Dressed in silk from head to toe, she floated like a glamour queen through the airport and led me to a luxurious car. Her apartment overlooked the bay and was lavishly furnished. It had wall-to-wall everything.

We settled in for a quick "hello" before dinner. She then took me to an exquisite restaurant down the street, where we dined on the terrace. Filet mignon, salad, asparagus with cream sauce, expensive Bordeaux, and a cognac with coffee for dessert.

After our next stint on the king-size bed, I could contain myself no longer.

"Irene, what the hell's going on? Did someone die and leave you a fortune?"

"Don't sweat it. You supported me for three months. Now it's my turn."

I agreed not to discuss the situation further, but it was all too mysterious.

The phone rang. Irene had a brief conversation and hung up.

"I have to go out for a while," she said. "Won't be long. Help yourself to drinks, TV, whatever."

"Irene, it's one o'clock in the morning. Where the hell are you going?" I was getting a tad worried.

"I'll be back soon."

It was light outside when she crept into bed. I turned to her but she was already asleep.

I rolled out around ten to find Irene in the kitchen on the phone, drinking coffee.

"Sleep well?" she asked, covering the mouthpiece and motioning toward the percolator. I poured a cup and looked around. In the light of day, the apartment seemed even more flamboyant and luxurious. My fears returned with a vengeance.

Irene whispered into the phone. "I'll be there. Right, I know." She hung up and eased over to me. She wrapped me in a kiss.

The next hour or so was a blur of eroticism. I would have given anything to bottle it for those cold winter nights that no doubt would arrive. Afterward, I started worrying again.

"You're going to have to tell me what's going on. It's uncomfortable being kept in the dark like this."

She rolled over and put on her robe.

"Why are you so goddamn nosy all of a sudden? What the hell's the difference? Can't you just enjoy it, and me?"

"Irene, it doesn't take a rocket scientist to figure out something's screwy. You've been here a little over two months, and you've earned enough to rent this palace, buy a wardrobe worth thousands of dollars and a car that costs more than a brain surgeon makes. Give me a break! Whatever you're doing has to be illegal, or very risky — or both."

I waited, hoping for a reply.

Irene softened and smiled.

"Let's not fight about it. I know what I'm doing. Look, tell you what, let's have a nice slow bath in that lovely tub. You know how I love to be bathed." Yes, indeed I did. "Then you can take the car and go for a drive while I see these people coming over for drinks and a chat."

She cooed and caressed, and of course I found myself in the tub. The subsequent rub-a-dub weakened my resolve. Before I left for my drive, I made her promise to tell me everything when I returned.

I visited some artist friends who were doing an early Florida show. Then I had lunch before heading back.

As I pulled into the parking lot, I was almost hit by a large black limousine that swerved only at the last minute, spitting gravel as it accelerated. I caught a quick glimpse of Irene in the back seat. She looked pale and frightened.

I let myself into the apartment. There was a note on the hall table. "Be back soon. Don't worry. Love." I left a brief reply on the bed, then packed my bags and took a taxi to the airport.

I was relieved to return to my moderate, conservative New England lifestyle. Irene's dark and shadowy existence had been shocking and scary.

About six months later, I was at a restaurant in the Tampa area. Friends were throwing a birthday party for me. We had eaten well and were moving to after-dinner drinks when the lights suddenly dimmed. A large cake burning with candles was carried in.

Amid the raucous birthday singing, I realised that the person carrying the cake was none other than Irene. My friends had arranged a surprise.

We stared at each other for a long moment in the midst of the clamor. She was as stunning as ever, and I was hard put not to sweep her off to a side room.

"Happy birthday, you bastard." She smiled and moved in for a monumental kiss that extinguished my candles.

Later, we took a stroll. She started crying as she struggled to get out the story. It came in a tumbling torrent of regret, remorse, anger, and fear. This beautiful woman was lost and alone with no one to care for her.

She told me that after returning to Florida from Canada, she realised that she did not have the skills to make money quickly. She turned to friends, who put her in touch with the owners of a massage parlour. Soon she graduated to more lucrative forms of personal attention. Her new employers installed her in the luxury apartment. She began using masses of drugs, provided free of charge. She did her best to persuade herself that the gig was temporary, just until she got on her feet.

It didn't take long until she was owned.

During the last few months, she had become a specialist in bondage and discipline, servicing the perversions of, among others, a judge, several national politicians, and numerous Mafia chiefs. Each flew in for weekly doses of Irene's punishment. In payment, she was well taken care of by her handlers.

I threw up my birthday dinner in a clump of bushes along the sidewalk.

Irene was in hysterics. She had seemed calm enough in the restaurant, but now I saw that she needed professional help. I told her I would do everything I could, and arranged to meet her at a discreet spot the following morning. Formulating a plan in my mind, I thought to take her north with me and try to repair the damage.

I realised this would be risky. The kind of people she was involved with don't take kindly to having their property stolen. I put her in a cab and reassured her that I would work things out.

Next day, I waited at our rendezvous spot for over two hours. I never saw her again.

I pray she escaped, but I realise it's a shallow prayer.

54

Blind Artists and Circus Clowns

A rt for art's sake is a lofty, noble aspiration. The ideal should never be forgotten. One must, however, keep eating. For that reason, itinerant painters are driven to paint something that will appeal to those who can afford to buy it.

In the United States, we have an enormous middle class with disposable funds for fun things. Purchased casually by many homeowners are giant screen TVs; sleek automobiles with excessive gasoline consumption; houses with three toilets; 127 pairs of socks; weekly visits to therapy/aerobics/golf/mistresses/lovers; double-door refrigerators that produce crushed ice; CDs; VCRs; and — occasionally — paintings to hang over the couch.

As a producer of things that hang over couches, I have been fortunate (seduced would perhaps be more apt) to have tapped into this well of loose change. It's kept me out of the poor house. At times I've been forced to a diet of baked beans, but never for long. Thank God I've never had to drink wine from a screwtop bottle.

It's been fairly good pickings. After all, new houses are built at an alarming rate. The average U.S. citizen moves every two years or more. New walls that need paintings and other decorations appear on the scene hourly.

Selling anything even vaguely artistic is a lofty occupation. It requires a subtle blend of pomposity, knowledge, and used-car salesmanship. Hawking one's own paintings requires all the above, with the added capacity to put one's ego on hold. It's almost impossible to regard a sliver of your soul as merchandise.

It is essential to be able to endure the ultimate in client harassment. "But Marvin, will it match the wallpaper and our magenta rug?"

"Yeah, I like that. Now what's the best you can do for me, buddy?"

"I want it to go between the lamp and the stuffed head."

"Tell you what I'm going to do. I'll give you cash, cold cash. What'll it take, right now?"

"Tell him I never pay retail for anything in my life."

"Personally, I don't think it will do, but the wife wants it. So help me out here. What do I have to come up with?"

I could fill a book with insensitive remarks like this.

I once was painting at a show in Chattanooga when a bustling lady dripping with shopping bags put her face between me and the canvas.

"Honey, whatcha paintin'?"

"A picture, madame."

"Sure, but what is it?"

"At the moment not much. When I'm finished it will be a harbor scene."

"Oh. What are those things there?"

"Masts."

"Mayersts? What the hell's thaert?"

"The pole to which sails are attached."

After a reflective pause: "They look like dead trees."

The idea of painting from one's memory, or inner vision, really bothers many people. They cannot conceive that whilst standing at one's easel outside a toy store in a mall in St. Petersburg, one can produce a rural landscape of southern France.

There is a great temptation to beat them at their own game.

"What kind of painting is that?"

"A great one."

"Did you go to school for this?"

"No, but I took a two-week correspondence course from the Divine Guidance School of Art in Palo Alto."

"You do this for a living?"

"No. I'm a brain surgeon. This is just a hobby."

"Will this painting be worth a lot of money someday?"

"Yes, when I'm dead. And I should tell you, I'm not feeling real great at the moment."

From '74 to '84, I travelled with several different outfits that organized art exhibits in shopping malls. I travelled in trailers and motor homes from Miami to Montreal, St. Petersburg to St. Louis, Atlanta to Green Bay.

There was very little if any "art," and a total absence of anything cultural. The shows were designed to make money, clear and simple. There were times I became very upset with the blatant disregard for artistic standards in these shows. Ethics went out the window when dollars were around. The ongoing policy was, "If it sells, it's good. If it doesn't, it's bad."

I had heated debates with many of the other artists about this, but I gave up after a time. They merely viewed me as far too sensitive and academic in my thinking. Others in the shows thought of me as likable but misguided. Dollars ruled the day. Art was a cover. "Everything boils down to a sale," we were told over and over.

Frankly, many of the artists on tour were little more than charlatans. I believe strongly that artists, and professionals in every field, ultimately must judge their actions by how they feel about "the face in the mirror." An artist can make a good living passing off a sham, but every dishonesty reflects in the soul. I've known artists who became stooped over after time, shoulders hunched, aged beyond their years-all because of their own unending "little lies."

The untruths of an artist may seem minor. Certainly this is not life-and-death stuff. We're not heart surgeons. But integrity is as important to an artist as it is to a physician or a banker. The years take a toll, and when a person cannot look back through the decades and feel good about himself, what has he really earned?

One story in particular sums up the disregard for honesty and integrity among some artists, and art shows in particular.

While on tour, our group was informed that the center spot for the day was going to be allocated to a "Blind Artist." We waited to see what would turn up to fill this absurd situation.

A great crowd of onlookers gathered. They didn't walk through the displays, looking at the art. They were there to see the blind artist. Sure enough, as though to a drum roll, a blind elderly lady was led out and seated before an easel. She proceeded to daub paint from prearranged pans onto wood panels. Her only guide was a series of pins laid out in a prearranged pattern.

Her colours were meaningless, haphazard. She sold out on the first day of the show. The other artists and I were left to reflect on the meaning of our lot.

55

Art with a Small a

There are three kinds of artists, four if you include house painters. Let's confine ourselves to the first three, although I have known some house painters who were damn fine artists.

First there are the kind who have produced paintings that you find selling at auction houses worldwide for sums that would keep most of us in resplendent luxury for the remainder of our lives (along with our children and children's children). These are major works by dead artists usually vaguely French. Picassos, Monets, Van Goghs, Renoirs, and Cezannes change ownership at alarmingly frequent intervals-with equally alarming price tags.

Truth is, they have ceased to be paintings. Along the rocky road of time and providence, they have been elevated to the category of investment. They are expected to show a healthy return that keeps pace with the rest of one's portfolio.

For an artist who is currently alive and working, this High End Art is a constant burr in the butt. A spot of burnt umber dead center in the titanium white.

It seems unfair that long-dead artists who have lived their lives and drank from their cups should be making more money than God. They have no use for it, after all. Meanwhile, we the living slug it out trying to make enough to buy the next meal and an extra tube of paint.

The second category includes artists producing paintings carried in the plethora of Legitimate Art Galleries. This is a diaphanous artistic umbrella. You will find paintings displayed in galleries everywhere, from swanky boulevards to tacky malls. These establishments spring up like weeds — and often are as quickly gone. Being retail establishments, they usually depend on good fortune. If they make it, fine. If not, the owner can always borrow more money and open a deli.

These galleries range from those that are conscientiously making an attempt to sell quality work by good artists, to those owned by retired insurance agents who need something to fill their daytime hours so they won't feel unduly depressed drinking themselves unconscious before the television every evening.

The art on display in these locations ranges from excellent to appalling. In this respect, art reflects life. Conveniently, the enormous well-fed middle class has tastes that also range from excellent to appalling, so it all works out just fine. Everyone gets what he wants.

Almost everyone. The artist invariably is left selling barely enough to cover framing costs. Why this is so, I have no idea.

Now we come to the third group, of which I was a card-carrying member for many years. Of course, there are no such things as cards for artists. Never has been, never will be. We could no more organise than fly to the back side of the moon. We're our own worst enemies.

This group comprises the souls who have chosen to embark on the precipitous journey of the wayfaring artist. They are at the low end of the artistic marketplace, along with the fruit and vegetables, pots and pans, and women's lingerie.

Wayfaring artists will travel anywhere and make any sacrifice to show their wares. Parking lots, malls, recreation facilities, dimly lit public lavatories — the artists will be there if a profit can be turned. On any given weekend across the length and breadth of our country there will be countless local fairs, clam bakes, and church bazaars. There the artists arrive with their travelling show and set up shop for one or two days. Well before the show is over they will be figuring where they will do the next one, how much gas it will take, and which interstate has the lowest tolls.

They long for a leg up. The next platform. A higher octave. Generally, they are a disgruntled lot, and who can blame them? They have the thankless task of having to appear professional and credible, just like "real" artists as seen in the glossy magazines and art periodicals. But it all rings hollow when push comes to shove.

There are probably tens of thousands of artists in this group splattered all over the fifty states. Only a small percentage have real talent. The majority are technicians who have stumbled on a formula that allows them to produce something that loosely fits under the general heading of art. Their product sells to hang on a wall and match the decor.

Where does that leave me?

By now, I am nothing if not a realist. I fit somewhere between the first two categories. I know myself well enough. The level of High End Art probably is unattainable, at least during my lifetime. I am unable to kiss enough arses, attend enough cocktail parties, and say enough right things to the right people at the right times in the right places.

There are those artists, I should say, who do this very well.

What we have then, is two distinct entities. The higher, which summons whispering down the wind to every artist, is the upper reach of artistic endeavour: the High End Art, populated by Picassos and Van Goghs. The lower is the commercial pipeline that distributes the great mass of everything else deemed artistic. It is the bread and butter of the great mass of artistic craftspersons, dabblers, and undiscovered geniuses.

The problem is, the edges between artists in these two echelons becomes blurred. Some artists doomed to work in the commercial pipeline have more artist talent and originality than those in High End Art. Conversely, and you can take this to the bank, there are artists whose work regularly sells at the auctions for millions who couldn't paint their way out of a toilet. Time will expose these, stamping their works with truth.

However, any of these options beats washing dishes.

I have been there.

56

Spring Street

E ver get the feeling that you're marking time? Spinning your wheels? Spending days without any definition, structure or purpose?

Round about the fall of 1976, I had a few days like that. Bothersome, worrying days. They made the mornings hard to get hold of. When the second cup of coffee didn't do anything for me, I knew something was up.

A good reason had to be lurking somewhere in my soul. After an afternoon of serious searching and a few tots of good port, I reached a not altogether surprising conclusion. I decided that spending my time wandering from mall to mall in an enormous trailer was not a terribly satisfying existence.

Things certainly could have been worse. I had a few bob in my pocket and was doing something that at least made use of my artistic training. I could eat a steak dinner now and then without feeling guilty. And I could read a wine list without skimming through to the house offering.

My paintings, however, were becoming decidedly dull. Whenever a work sold, I had to replace it quickly to continue the flow of funds. I was grateful for having the luxury to consider this a dilemma, but it was beginning to rankle.

How many sailboats can an artist produce in a month? How many regattas, wharves, trawlers, and New England barns?

By then, I could paint them all in my sleep. I was making little headway into the more serious and prestigious echelons of the art world. And again I was being nagged by the questions that had caused me to leave my job at the London graphic design agency so many years before. When would I strive to reach my depths as an artist? When would I make the effort to reach inside and express deeper feelings and perceptions?

By now it was quite obvious that the organizers of the tour had little interest in expanding or refining the shows. They were focused on the weekly take. Quality and calibre had all but gone out the window. It seemed irrelevant to them. One new member of our travelling circus made it quite clear that his paintings were actually photographs on canvas, which he touched up with inarticulate daubs of paint and tacked into gaudy gold frames. He sold them by the bucket full. The organizers loved it!

It was disillusioning to the old guard. We had worked hard to establish a marketplace; now it was being misused. Our expectations had been ill-founded. As the saying goes,"Put not thy trust in princes...."

Just as I had these thoughts, the idea of moving to New York flashed through my mind. New York, as someone once noted, "is where they give out the prizes." It's also the heart and generator of the contemporary art world. It has been described as Rome in decline, Athens with an attitude, and turn-of-the-century Paris gone stark raving mad.

That was for me. The Big Apple. The place to flex one's artistic muscles. One gets the feeling that "they" know about art there.

Having managed to put away a little money for the inevitable rainy day, I persuaded myself that the stormclouds had arrived. I decided that the money would be well spent acquiring a loft in Soho, the then-current art center of the universe.

It took about a month of footslogging the area between Houston and Canal before I found a dream loft on the third floor of a desirably seamy building. It was on Spring Street, just up from West Broadway. Three hundred a month with big windows overlooking the bustling street, and big cockroaches overlooking nothing.

My first encounter with New York mentality served as a fitting prelude. Before moving into the loft, I had to remove the junk and old furniture left by previous tenants. Arriving early on the morning I was to move in, I parked my rusty old van outside the front entrance of the building. I lugged trash, debris, old furniture, and mammoth nonfunctional appliances out of the apartment and down to the street. Hauling them off myself to a dump in the countryside would sidestep the outrageous fees the city charged for the service.

As noontime arrived, I was struggling with the final item, a large, incredibly heavy stove of 1940 vintage. It was almost impossible to move across the sidewalk. I slid it inch by inch. A few more feet and I would be able to lever it into the back of the van.

Just then Mr. Warmth, a street cop, sauntered across the avenue. He looked down at me as I grappled with the monster. "Dis ya van?" What an accent. Did he have a mouthful of meatballs?

"I'll be out of your way if I can just manage to get this damn thing into the back," I said. "Perhaps you would be kind enough to give me a hand?"

He looked at me as though I'd made an indecent proposal. "Hey, buddy, move the goddamn vehicle."

"I really am doing my best to oblige." I was getting a tad pissed off.

"Hey, buddy, like right now!"

My patience snapped. Sweat poured from every pore of my body. My adrenaline buzzed like a Grand Prix auto with a blown cylinder. I lifted the appliance with an almighty heave and flung it up into the back. It slid out again, falling on my foot, pinning it to the pavement.

I screamed in pain. Two passersby jumped forward and helped me lift the stove back inside.

Blood trickled right through my shoe onto the pavement. The cop stood flat footed, staring with his fat mouth open.

"Hey, buddy, ya gonna move this friggin thing or what?"

"First, my dear sir, I am not and never will be your 'buddy.' Second, I may well have broken my foot. Third, you must be confusing me with someone who gives a shit at this particular moment!"

I slammed the rear doors and dragged my throbbing foot into the driver's seat. As I started to pull from the curb, the cop moved alongside.

"Hey, asshole, you gonna move this?"

We now know why murders occur. I doubt seriously the man died a natural death.

I raced up the FDR at over thirty miles an hour and finally found a dump that would allow me to unload.

My foot took a month to heal.

57

Smog and Boa Constrictors

L ife in the Big Apple was a lot different from camping in
a trailer. New York was a don't-mess-with-me-buddy city
that had no patience for anyone who couldn't stand the
pace. The weak were pushed to the side to make room for the
other contestants. It was a loud, whirling, madcap place with
no quarter given or taken.

It was also an extremely expensive place to live. I used up
my rainy day funds establishing myself and my loft. Almost
immediately upon getting settled, I was obliged to seek income.

I made contact with an "uptown" art dealer. There is no
reason to pollute these pages with a description of the inequi-
ties suffered by artists at the hands of these scumbags posing
as beneficiaries to the art world. At best, they may be regarded
as nonentities who exist by the systematic exploitation of any
worthy soul who happens to fall into their clutches.

I was in the unenviable position of needing cash. That was
music to their ears, and I soon found myself painting quite large
canvasses for a hundred bucks a pop. It paid the rent and put
food on the table, but did they care about an especially expressive passage I had achieved? About an unusually fine juxtapo-
sition of harmonies? About anything worthwhile at all?

Walking home the first night, I was sure that everyone I
passed knew I was prostituting myself. I felt as though I had

pulled my pants down at rush hour.

Within a month, I was living an existence as constipating as when I had been on the road. I continued to pass the posh Soho galleries each day, salivating at the thought of one day having my own show. It did seem a long way off.

New York can be the loneliest of places. Even in the midst of one of the most artistic locales this side of Montmartre, I found myself living a singularly solitary existence. I made few friends, which was unusual for me. My existence was becoming as thrilling as a trainee monk undergoing vows of celibacy, poverty, fasting, and silence.

I stuck it out, convinced that things would brighten up.

They didn't.

I spent a somber Christmas shared with an equally lonely and depressed friend. We ate a large dinner, drank some heavenly wine, watched Alistair Sim in *A Christman Carol*, and retired early.

Hell of a Christmas. One of my worst.

On the whole, come spring, I was ready to call it quits.

I rejoined my touring friends for a brief spell, but my absence had not endeared me to the tour directors. They regarded me as something of a traitor, having aspired to the legitimate theater of art. I was treated as a newcomer. My spaces in the shows were assigned appropriately — dead arse end of each mall.

No one likes a renegade.

I returned to New York for one last try. By then, it was full summer. Temperatures in the city were inching upward. One afternoon, sometime in mid-August, I was trying to finish an order for my uptown dealers. I had all the windows flung open and as many fans going as I could lay my hands on. Air conditioning was out of the question. The antiquated wiring would not handle it. The heat was oppressive. I was drenched from head to foot. I was down to my underwear, but the sweat still poured in torrents. My feet felt as though they were standing in a shallow pool.

I had inherited one of those indoor/outdoor thermometers attached to a window. It was 95 degrees outside, 102 inside.

Out in the street, the usual throb of traffic droned continuously. Sirens wailed. On the rooftop opposite, pigeons congregated for a strategy session. "You take Fifth Street, Charley. I'll handle Broadway. Let's do lunch." The haze of heat blotted out the sun and muffled the din. I swallowed another gallon of water and pressed on. It was so humid the paint refused to dry. An enormous eighteen-wheel semi pulled to a red light at the corner of Spring and Wooster, just below my third-floor perch. The light changed, and the driver gunned his enormous engine. Amid the deafening roar, a pall of black diesel smoke drifted in through my window. The oily smoke hung in the loft as if a bomb had exploded. The smell choked me. Black granules of soot started to drift down, settling on my painting.

That was the final straw.

I threw a few things into a bag, hailed a cab and headed for La Guardia. I caught the first plane to Nantucket and spent the next few days floating in the delightful salt water. Only at the end of September did I return to the loft to collect and sell my belongings. It was 1978, and I was off to new adventures.

Hindsight is always 20/20. I let the lease of that prime piece of real estate on Spring Street go to an eccentric uptown psychiatrist for ten grand. If you could find a loft like it now, the rent alone would be close to eight thousand a month. Purchasing a lease would probably entail your first born. If I still had the space, I could probably retire on the proceeds of the sale.

But I was so disillusioned at the time that I would have paid for the privilege of moving out.

There is an interesting postscript to the story. About two years after I left, the owner of the Spring Street building contacted me. At some point, the psychiatrist who had bought my lease had begun acting quite oddly — a not uncommon occurrence for people in his line of work, I suppose.

It seemed that before moving from the loft, he had imported several boa constrictors as pets. He left the snakes, which bred like rabbits. Tenants all over the building found themselves deluged by the slithery creatures, which quite handily made their way through nooks and crannies in the old walls. The building was infested, and the owner wanted to know if I could tell him where the psychiatrist was.

The owner didn't say exactly what he wanted to discuss with the good doctor.

58

Resurrection in Nantucket

I had discovered Nantucket in 1974, when invited to exhibit at one of the island's galleries. That was my first one-man show in the United States. I immediately fell in love with the island's ambience. Life there was refreshing, and certainly the closest thing to a European flavour that I had encountered in the States. I felt immediately at home. There were no skyscrapers, no interstates, not even a traffic light on the nine-by-fifteen mile strip of land. Day-to-day living was slow, quiet, and ordered — much as in my beloved Ramatuelle.

This exquisite little island about twenty-five miles south of Cape Cod has had a checkered career. It was settled some four hundred years ago by a few stray Pilgrims from England who saw a chance to set down roots. They did a good job and by the 1800s found themselves with a thriving port and one of the world's largest whaling fleets. Commerce flourished until some myopic soul discovered profitable uses for fossil fuel and set in motion the industrial plague that has all but finished us off.

Nantucket faired badly in the transition. Whale oil lost favor, and the little island fell into decline. It became forgotten until around the 1920s, when the well-heeled and affluent, always looking for a place to escape the ravenous elegance of wealth and society, descended on the island and transformed it into a fashionable retreat. As the years rolled along, it be-

219

came an elitist paradise. Winters are raw, but summers are glorious, and come June, ferries from the mainland are thronged by vacationers escaping to their summer homes. Whaling vessels are rarely spotted these days in the island's ports; the economy is fueled by tourism and property taxes.

Few, other than land developers and local politicians, would say that the change has been for the better. Nonetheless, the move to Nantucket was one of the wisest I've made. For six years previously, my finest paintings had drawn inspiration from the fabulously beautiful views of southern France. The atmosphere of such locales invites relaxation and comfort. For me, the joy of life is expressed in such paintings.

Wonder of wonders, Nantucket galleries were looking for just such works. The wealthy vacationers arriving each spring needed paintings for their houses and yachts. They did not want dreary pieces. They wanted paintings that celebrate the happiness life can offer. They'd had enough of bleak winters and grey offices. They wanted expansiveness and freedom. That is what my paintings offered, and they were well received. Soon, I found local Nantucket vistas that offered comparable scope: yachts at rest, boats with sails billowing, panoramas of shoreline and bright, happy sky.

During my first summer on the island, from June to August 1978, I sold paintings through a local gallery. I had to continue with the increasingly tacky but still lucrative Mall Tour through May 1979. I then hurried down to the ferry and floated over to Nantucket for a summer of warmth and vigorous work at my easel. The days were smooth and the ocean breezes balmy. My work, I felt, was coming into maturity. Again represented by a local gallery, I sold my paintings almost as quickly as I could produce them.

59

Farewell to the Malls

I n the late eighties, I came to the conclusion that it was time to find a different road. Summers in Nantucket were wonderful, but winters hawking my wares in Florida malls and parking lots were taking its toll on body and spirit. I was earning a reasonable living, but needed to head for the next level.

In December 1988, I received notification that I had been accepted to exhibit at the Coconut Grove Art Show the following February. This event had maintained eminent standards through the years and had always attracted talented artists. It was a highly coveted show in which to exhibit, so I prepared for it with anticipation.

That year proved to be the beginning of the show's decline. The plethora of mass-produced craft items, and bad paintings reduced the exhibit to an embarrassment. Coconut Grove was jammed. The blistering and steamy three days became a swarming, beer-guzzling, raucous street bash.

The artists were relieved when it was over.

Sitting alone in my Miami hotel room, the bottle of cognac quickly disappearing, I suddenly realized that since enrolling in the strange and wonderous world of itinerant art purveyor to the great unwashed, I had been the sole proprietor of my business. As such, I was obliged to wear a dizzying variety of hats.

I produced the merchandise — in this case original paintings. I wholesaled them to galleries, print stores, and framing shops to be resold at heavy mark-ups. (Of course one never looks in the other guy's pocket.) I also retailed them in the summer months on Nantucket and in the various shows at which I exhibited. I was responsible for marketing, PR, and all related press and media contact. On top of this, I took care of framing, packing, crating, and shipping.

A complex manufacturing concern! Dare I say it, a substantial business. I was, in fact, a one-man band rapidly running out of steam for the blowing of the trumpet and the banging of the drum and cymbals.

Finding an art publisher that would represent my work seemed to be the key for a person such as myself to rise through the ranks. These are organizations that contract artists to work with them. The artist produces original paintings, and the art publisher makes silkscreen and lithographic prints, which the company then distributes through a network of outlets. The more scrupulous publishers actually pay the artist a stipend and a royalty.

The artist is marketed and promoted. The nuts and bolts of life are taken care of, allowing the artistic soul to focus exclusively on work. With luck, and if the market holds, the artist may in time reach the upper end of the commercial art industry. Then, who knows? His work might become a desirable property and end up at an auction house, or hang in the uptown galleries. In short, the artist may become famous.

I had been informed that the International Art Expo held each spring in New York was the best place to catch such a big fish. When I inquired about the cost of a small booth at the Expo, I was staggered. Five thousand dollars! That didn't include the cost of crating and shipping my paintings, nor travel and lodging. I had managed to save a little, but five thousand may as well have been one hundred thousand.

Still in Miami, with February 1989 barely two and a half months away, I made a decision. Showing at the next Art Expo was out of the question. There simply was not time to gather the money-nor prepare enough first-class pieces.

I set the goal to attend the Expo and catch my big fish the

following year, in March 1990. What's more, I steeled myself to achieve a higher level of artistic creation by that time. I vowed never again to work on a painting that did not engage my finest sensibilities. I had not compromised unduly while traveling on the Mall Circuit, but to be honest I had hardly reached deeply inside to my artistic source. Even my recent paintings of Nantucket, which were much nearer my heart, had been created with a sort of Mall-Circuit mentality. I knew that to contract with an established art publisher, I would have to paint at a higher level than I had been used to, and then paint on that level consistently.

I decided to finish my commitment for the winter with the Florida Mall Circuit. That would give me enough money to set up for the start of summer 1989 and prepare for spring 1990. I told myself that once on the island in June, I would not leave until going to New York the following March. This meant that I had to make enough money to spend the winter of 1989-90 on Nantucket — without the income received from the winter Mall Circuit.

To follow through with this do-or-die was not unlike many moves I had made before. This, however, seemed different. I had honed my craft. And I couldn't make a leap to the next level spending my days in malls.

When June arrived, I returned to the island and went straight at it, painting day and night. I rented a small gallery and lived on premises, just as I had so many years before in Ramatuelle after leaving my job in London. My social life dropped off to nothing. I had no money to spend anyway. Through June and July, I hardly sold a painting. Not many people even wandered into my little gallery. That was fine with me. More time to work with undivided attention.

For the first time in years, I threw away paintings that did not meet my new vision. These were complete, finished pieces that I could have sold in the malls. I wanted more. I wanted expression.

Reaching inside to the finest times in my life, I painted St. Tropez harbour scenes and sweeping Mediterranean coastlines. The latter, in particular, allow stunning contrasts of colour and hue. Foregrounds can be painted with clarity, capturing the particularly crystalline quality of Mediterranean light. Middle grounds can be painted less distinctly, emphasizing the sparkling water and the shimmering loveliness of cascading hillside villas. Distances can be softer still, with far mountains sloping to meet the shore in a hazy blueness of salt air.

Throughout the summer I worked in the brilliant Nantucket air, producing works of colour, brightness, and bouncing light. September approached; the season was winding down. With my focus on creation and artistic development, my summer sales had slipped terribly. I was down to my last several hundred dollars, with the entire winter before me. Soon there would be no seasonal tourists, no buyers whatsoever. Time was running out on me.

60
Nantucket Gallery

L ate August. It had been a slow day at the Hallam Gallery. I'd been sitting listlessly behind the desk in the tiny fisherman's shack at the end of the Wharf for most of the morning. A world-famous film star had been dragged in by his wife, a well-known model. He didn't like the frames, so they left to continue their "low profile" vacation. The high spot of the afternoon was when a dog sneaked in and threatened to lift his leg on the corner display.

Every summer from May to September the wealthy and famous come to Nantucket to show off the latest in yachts and jewelry. The year-round community of ten thousand temporarily swells to forty thousand as the deluge descends on the tiny island.

The locals regard these interlopers as a necessary but unwelcome ingredient to their lives. Year-round inhabitants would much prefer vacationers to simply wire their holiday money to island banks and remain in their mainland mansions. There is little justice in this life. Every summer, island residents are obliged to hand over their quiet sanctuary. But needs must be met. Without the tourists, winter would be a gloomy prospect. Cold winds would blow and there would be no money for cable TV and the vital ingredients of hot toddies.

Summer sales had hardly improved with the coming of September. I was beginning to wonder if my plan was blowing up in my face. I was approaching the age of fifty, but things could have been worse. There was a lot for which to be thankful. I had good health, tennis at the local courts, and I was doing what I loved to do more than anything: paint.

Not bad. Not bad at all.

And yet. . . .

Ah well, anyone can have a moment's nostalgia. Memories of the past. A thought of what might have been. Friends long gone. Lovers not to be forgotten.

A little tiredness, perhaps. I closed the gallery, climbed into my car and decided to let it take me where it would.

We ended up at the beach, where I strolled to the edge of the dunes and gazed out at the summer scene. Children scampered about the sand, whooping and screaming as the tide washed around the base of their sand castles. Mothers languished in the shade of multicolored umbrellas. Husbands had hushed conversations on their cellular phones, unable to sever the corporate umbilical cord. Seagulls swooped and dived; beachballs floated on the waves; dots of sailboats speckled the blue waters of the bay; wind surfers galloped over the white plumes; rock music crackled from boomboxes; picnic lunches were spread over blankets; and a gentle breeze fanned the scene with the perfumes of suntan oil.

I sank into a dune and basked in the tranquility of the moment. A tiny young girl with blonde hair and tanned skin wobbled up to me and offered her beachball. I took it from her and threw it back toward the water. She gurgled after it and returned to the safety of her family.

I decided to give myself over to the spirit of the beach, lying back and letting the hot sunshine permeate and soothe my mind. I dozed off into a gentle sleep, lulled by the lapping of the sea.

The evening shift at the gallery was quiet. Only a few strollers passed through. It was as though everyone on the island was experiencing the same quiet inner nostalgia that I was.

The evening dragged along, and I was preparing for an early close when a teenage girl walked in. She wanted to buy something for her father's birthday and thought that a painting of Nantucket would be perfect.

She didn't have much money, so I showed her a few of my watercolour sketches. She liked them and chose a piece. She knew her mind, I'll say that for her. When she saw what she wanted, she bought it straightaway.

It was a small sale, but it made me feel that the day had not been an entire waste. As I was about to close, she returned with her father. He was a tall, distinguished-looking man in his fifties with the easy manner particular to those who are well set and well fed.

They strolled around the gallery. I pretended to bury myself in paperwork as I watched them. I liked their body language. They were liking what they saw.

The man turned to me and spoke with an authoritative air. He was used to saying something once and once only. "I like this, this, this, this, that one, this here, that, those two and the three there. Oh this, and this and those two there. Give me a price for all of them."

Saying this, he strolled outside to talk with friends.

Stunned, I began to total the prices of the paintings, as he had asked. The group stood outside, laughing and talking. I estimated that if this was a serious proposal, it would not only take care of winter's expenses, it would allow me to pay for the booth at Art Expo in March. I scribbled the prices and arrived at a grand total, with a suitable accommodation for the size of the purchase.

The gentleman came back into the gallery.

"So what do the numbers look like?"

I showed him the paper, trying to make it seem as though this was an everyday occurrence for me.

He studied it.

"Right. It's a deal. Bring them to my boat, if you would. I'll send up one of my guys to help."

He pulled out his checkbook. Oh, that most beautiful of objects. He had purchased fourteen paintings.

Later, we had drinks on his floating palace and chatted about this and that. He was "in oil" and needed the paintings for his homes in Florida, Italy, London, and Hong Kong.

"Knew the minute I saw them they were perfect. Good work!"

Next morning, still feeling slightly numb, I was at the gallery early. The gentleman "in oil" walked in. He literally entered with checkbook in hand.

"I think I need a couple more for the boat."

He chose two more pieces.

"Oh, and that small watercolour. I'd like to give it to my daughter as a souvenir of our trip to Nantucket."

That afternoon I mailed off a check for the booth and reserved a hotel room. Then I closed the gallery for the day and went back to play sandcastles on the beach.

The impossible had become reality.

61

Daybreak

There's a spot I go to watch the morning arrive,
Near the beach where the old boats go to die.
There they lie, holes in their bows, rotted and rusted,
On the shore of that unwanted forgotten spot.
It's a good place for sitting though.
I've never seen another soul there.
This is the time of day worth getting up for.
At five-thirty the world is still, tranquil, restful.
It is a time of quiet thoughts and solitude.
The dizzying trumpet of the day has not yet tuned
    up.
The dawn is pure, the morning breath soft.
The sun, always on time, peeks through and nudges
    away mists cocooning the silent streets and shingle
    houses.
Boats languish at anchor, awaiting a breeze to renew
    their spirit.
What is life for a boat with no wind?
The millpond harbour catches a twinkle of silver, a
    glisten of gold.
Gulls diving into the waves celebrate wakefulness.

The lighthouse's plaintive foghorn bounces over the
  bay.
The lighthouse doesn't like seagulls-never has.

This morning, amid the broken boats and rotted
  hulls,
My thoughts are of mists and fogs.
The great pea-souper of '57, in London.
For two days the city smelled of sulphur and old
  socks.
A Scottish fog swirling around the muffled wail of a
  pipe band near Loch Ness.
A sudden bank of swirling mist on the way home
  from a sailing holiday near Cherbourg.
I have seen a fog or two.
They can drop like a curtain, obliterating everything.
They're fogs that catch in your soul.
Yet the sun always wins in the end. It has a perfect
  record.
Today, the mist will probably burn off by ten.
I'll walk away from this dead old beach
Into a warm day filled with seaside scuffles and
  billowing sails.
Years from now, I'll remember this morning.
I'll remember the fog easy to escape,
And the broken boats easy to walk away from.
If only my own fog could lift so easily,
And shadows of the past vanish in the rising light.

62

Nude with Nor'easter

A week or so later, I was getting ready to close the gallery to get home in time for the evening news. As had become my custom after the large sale and the reservation of my booth, I was spending all my free time painting. I found myself doing almost as much thinking about my work as actually putting brush to canvas. I knew that I had time to prepare as many pieces as I would need for March. The important thing was to make certain that each piece was at the highest level I could produce.

An attractive couple had been looking around the gallery for ten minutes or so. They finally decided on two paintings: a three-panel triptych and a regatta. They were polite and pleasant. We had no trouble agreeing on a price for the two.

The couple radiated confidence, as though telling the world in a subtle but definite way that they didn't need to prove anything to anyone. Talking with them, I learned that their names were David and Elisa. They lived in a well-groomed area of Connecticut and had just finished building a large home on Nantucket.

Elisa was quite dazzling, in her early thirties, exquisitely dressed, with a bubbling, effervescent personality. "Do you do figure work?" she asked in a rather secretive manner, though

231

they were the only customers in the gallery.

I explained that I enjoyed painting nudes from time to time, provided that the model had an interesting figure and a good personality. I emphasized that I didn't do many of them because it was not a subject matter that sold well. "People are still intimidated by the human figure, especially unclothed," I explained, wondering if the statement would put them off.

Not a bit. They wanted a nude on a beach, 60" x 90", to adorn the wall above the bed. The figure, they said, should look like Elisa a decade or so earlier, before she had been swept into the holy state by her husband — and before gravity and luxurious living had taken a small toll around the edges.

I must say that I was warming to the idea of painting Elisa in her altogether, but it was quickly explained that I would not have the opportunity, appealing to her though it was (smile and eyelash flutter).

No. It would be preferable to find a local model. Thinking of the tanned young college girls still festooning the island, I figured it would be no problem soliciting the help of one for a quick pose and a cup of tea one afternoon.

The first girl I approached gave me a look intended to turn me to stone. Over the next few days, during which I approached at least a dozen other girls, my proposal was met either with polite humor (I was obviously trying a new line) or definite anger (I had made an indecent proposal).

This was not going to be as easy as I had imagined. What had happened to the world? Where would Renoir, Picasso, Matisse, and every old master since the year 1500 have been without a few females willing to bare all in the name of art?

After an exhaustive search, I settled for a not altogether unattractive girl who was unfortunately as thin as a bean pole. She was brunette (Elisa was blonde) and ill at ease with the body she had been issued.

After a couple of hours working with her on the beach, I had what I thought would be a set of useful drawings from which to operate. I paid her off, and she took the money with obvious relief. For her, the two hours had been utterly boring.

A week later I had the nearly completed painting on my easel. I wasn't altogether happy with it. It seemed somewhat contrived. The model floated above the sand no matter what I did with the colour or design. The dune grass looked like dried straw. The beach itself had the appearance of a concrete parking lot, and the sea resembled cold porridge. I broke out in a cold sweat every time I worked on it.

Finally, I concluded that I could try from now till doomsday and not improve the painting an iota. So, satisfied with it or not, I would have to deliver it and risk rejection.

I signed the painting and enclosed it in wrapping paper and several thick layers of plastic. The painting was too large to fit inside my van, so I made a large cardboard container that strapped on top. Catching an early ferry, I headed off in the direction of Connecticut. Halfway through Massachusetts, engine trouble forced me to stop. After a few hours in a garage, an astute mechanic figured out what was wrong. I had forgotten to put gas in the tank. As he condescendingly put it, an engine has a 70 to 80 percent better chance of working when it has some petrol. I called it a day and checked into a motel.

I bought some good rope and tethered my cargo to the top of the van for extra security. To ride out the evening, I also bought a bottle of good wine. During the night I heard rain. Very strong rain. But the painting was doubly wrapped in plastic, and cardboard makes a strong enough container.

I woke about six in the morning, regretting the consumption of wine, and gradually become aware that the rain had stopped. I showered, trying to clear my head, and set off for breakfast and coffee.

As I passed my van, I was pulled suddenly into full consciousness. My jaw dropped. The boxed painting was gone!

The remains of a few ropes hung in shreds down the sides of the van. Gazing up and down the parking lot, I thought I saw a piece of rope at the far end. Dashing the length of pavement, I saw that yes, it was a strand of my rope. I proceeded on, and as I rounded a corner I saw the painting. It was lodged about a third of the way up a tall tree. There were no signs of the cardboard box or wrapping.

Since the box had been extremely well constructed and fastened, and the wrapping had been securely taped and re-taped, how they detached from the painting without tearing the painting apart is a complete mystery.

It took about fifteen minutes to climb the tree. Tall and with limbs far apart, this was not a tree made for climbing. That, along with my aching head, made for quite a delightful morning.

Half an hour later, I had the painting free. I dropped it to the ground as gently as I could. Miraculously, there were only superficial markings, which I was able to repair fairly easily. Strapping it back on top of the van, I dashed in for a quick breakfast. Everyone was talking about the hurricane.

Hurricane?

Indeed, the hurricane that had blown through during the night. I hadn't known a thing about it. Farther down the coast, the wind had done considerable damage. Trees had been uprooted and powerlines downed. Even a few houses had been torn from foundations.

But my painting had done battle and survived. A litany to canvas, wood, and acrylic paint.

David and Elisa were delighted with the work. Placed on their wall, it seemed much improved from when in the studio. Paintings do that sometime.

As far as I know, it still hangs in their house. The cardboard box is listed as missing in action.

63
Art Expo

Having reserved what seemed to me an small, extremely expensive booth (a large one would have bankrupted me), I made arrangements to crate and ship the twenty or so pieces that I had selected to show. Filling out the required forms, brokerage manifests, and numerous other items sticky with red tape made the enterprise draining. I seemed suddenly to be dealing with people whose sole purpose in life was to bog me down.

I survived that first obstacle course and on a bitterly cold March day arrived in New York ready to take the unsuspecting Art World by storm. Immediately upon entering the exhibition hall, I came up against the second stumbling block.

Unions!

I have no quarrel with people who expect to be paid for doing their job, and who in the process desire fair, humane, and considerate treatment. Coming as I have from a working-class background, I am intimately familiar with the hopelessness and misery poverty can cause. There is a limit, however.

It became apparent from the outshot that the unions involved in the running of the huge conference/exhibition center had things completely under their rigid, uncompromising control. The idea, it seemed, was not to facilitate everyone else's commercial activities, but to hinder as much as humanly possible.

I needed a special union man to hammer in hooks on which to hang my paintings. I needed a second union man to actually lift the paintings onto said hooks. Then there were union men licensed to set up the lighting fixtures and screw in the bulbs (separate unions these, had to find two different people). I quickly ran afoul of this virulent regime when I tried to lift a box that was sitting in my display space. Two overweight, aggressive men with body odor and overhanging bellies waddled over and asked what the fuck did I think I was fucking doing with the fucking goddam box. I tried to explain that I needed to open it so that I could find the tools needed to set up my display. At the word 'tool' their combined blood pressure leaped into the red zone. I was treated to a fifteen-minute harangue on what would happen if I so much as touched a fucking hammer let alone tried to fucking use it. Fucking, goddam motherfrigging damn shithead balls.

I got the message. Standing perfectly still in one place, I could only point out what needed to be done as an army of cretins with one inch of forehead and breath like the arse end of a rabbit warren milled around my precious paintings.

With enormous willpower and a couple bottles of aspirin — and with considerable tongue biting — I managed to complete the display. I was at last ready for the show to begin.

Art Expo was an awe-inspiring exhibition featuring artists, sculptors, publishers, framemakers, and printmakers from all over the world. Buyers, sellers, gawkers, and artists bustled from booth to booth. Business, I suppose, is a lot like justice. Not only must it be done, it must appear to be done. There were over six miles of exhibits, and judging by the frenetic activity, business was being executed along every yard of the show.

Streams of people poured past my booth. Most glanced in my direction and walked past, so blitzed by the hectic atmosphere that they didn't register my presence. But from time to time an interested person stepped out of the flow for a closer look. Some talked and moved on, some bought a small piece, others bought substantially. It was obvious that my work was appreciated.

By the third and last day, I had sold enough of my original pieces to meet my expenses. I had made good contacts with a few galleries that expressed interest in doing shows with me in the near future. But I still had not hooked my big fish.

Late in the afternoon, I got involved in a rather shady deal with a gentleman who wanted to buy six of my pieces for cash. We had been dancing around on price for the best part of an hour, and it was getting close to the time when I needed to start breaking down my display (with of course help from the union brothers). We finally agreed on a price for the lot and started the delicate business of transferring funds. It was bewildering how many secret places this man had about his person. Tens, twenties, and hundreds were pulled from his jacket pockets, belt, trousers-even from his socks and shoes. What he was doing with all this cash I had no idea.

Finally the transaction was complete. He took the paintings and I was left with thousands of dollars in unmarked funds and no secret pockets in which to hide them. This was, of course, New York — and I didn't have a bodyguard or a gun.

There was only one thing to do: hide the loot in my pockets, leave the booth to its own devices, and make a beeline for the first taxi. I figured that if I didn't get mugged on the way, I could drop it all into the safe deposit at my hotel.

Standing suddenly in front of me, three representatives of one of the world's largest and most respected art publishers and distributors introduced themselves with a conservative air of professional cordiality. Pretending not to notice that I was stuffing money into every pocket I could find, they informed me that they had noticed my work during the show and were impressed, not only with its quality but by how well it was selling.

They glanced around my booth (still pretending not to notice the cash), checking out one of my larger acrylics still hanging on the divider. From my years of one-to-one selling in the malls, or from a natural artistic instinct, I had become able to tune myself to viewers of my art; almost as though seeing through their eyes. I looked at the painting and knew that they liked what they saw.

They picked up conversation again.

"How long had I been painting?"

"Had I gone to art school?"

"Really? How fine."

"Oh, you have a small gallery on Nantucket? Is that where you'll be going after the show?"

Then, quick glances among them. Unspoken group affirmation before proceeding:

"Would you be free to drop by our corporate offices during the next few days? We could perhaps discuss the possibility of signing a contract."

I was lightheaded. My lips began moving.

"Yes, indeed I would be free to drop by."

I was astonished by how casually these words came out. As though the entire affair was the most natural, everyday event. As though I had not scratched, clawed, starved, connived, protested, pretended, begged (never stolen, grateful to say), slogged, seethed, floundered, raged blindly, been humbled, been screwed royally, laboured with agony and generally sweated blood day and night for three decades to get to this unattainable moment.

Epilogue

"G oo moorin. Dis is you co-pirot speaki flom co-pit. We ar frying at firty fi fousan fee. Our estmati allivar in Tokyo is in firtee how and ferty mini."

The announcement sounds almost the same when the "co-pirot" repeats it in Japanese. I can't imagine why he bothers. No one can hear or understand a word he says. And do we really care what the temperature is in Tokyo? Or that there are clouds and light rain? By the time we get there it will doubtless have changed. I suppose it is all part of airline professional hygiene.

Nippon Airways does a good job, however. Hot and cold running 'fright' attendants all over the place just dying to bring you hot soup and the beverage of your choice. The flight from JFK to Narita is fourteen hours, good for at least a couple of bowls and a few bottles of plonk.

Being ensconced in the luxury of first class, with personal headphones, pillows, and blankets (in case honorable feet get cold), gives one an intense sense of superiority. I feel important. A man with serious stuff to do.

I am on my way to the land of sushi and squid for a twenty-city exhibition tour of my recent paintings and prints. It is the tenth such in the past five years. The publishing house with which I am affiliated arranges two of these tours each year.

They are usually very lucrative. This tour will take me the length and breadth of the country, from Tokyo all the way down to Fukuoka in Kyushu. No expense is spared. I will stay at some of the very best hotels, eat at the finest restaurants, and generally travel in style.

Things have been going exceptionally well the past five years, thanks to the expertise of my publisher. Shortly after the Art Expo at which I put together my pennies to rent a small booth, I signed a contract that has been worth a truly substantial amount of money. For the last five years I have painted nearly every day, producing thousands of acrylics and oils of all sizes. My publisher has sold each of these through its network of representatives and galleries, with hardly any doing on my part. In addition, many of my works have been made into the finest quality limited-edition serigraphs selling for quite fine prices.

Galleries from New York to San Francisco, from Tokyo to London carry my originals and prints. At a recent Art Expo in New York, my publisher rented more than fifty booths (and you know the cost of New York real estate these days). The rented area took up three or four complete aisles, over which were hung elaborate displays and originals and prints by myself and their other artists. I was the featured artist, with forty original pieces on display. Galleries and distribution organizations from the world over trooped through as I signed posters, chatted pleasantly and basked in the glory of the moment. This certainly was a contrast to the frantic, down-to-the-last-penny experience of only a few years before when I rented my little booth. I have come to realize the secret to artistic success: distribution!

Speaking objectively (always something of a stretch for an artist) I have arrived at the pinnacle of my professional career. I can gaze down at the litter and carnage of the bodies that have fallen, the flotsam of debris cast aside in the quest, and feel elated. I have arrived. I am here.

I can lay down my sword, remove my armor, take a deep breath, and eat my egg salad sandwich with satisfaction.

Replete with a defined benefit program, trust accounts, healthy bank balances, safe-deposit boxes full of goodies, cellphones, several houses, a spiffy automobile or two, wine in the cellar, steaks in the fridge, and a cleaning lady to tidy up after me, it's safe to say that I am well situated. I have no less than five toilets in which to take my daily constitutional. If that isn't success, what is? It's all relative, I know — but nonetheless comforting. My cup indeed runneth over.

In my quiet moments, I realise that the most lasting and significant benefit of all this — the all-encompassing blessing that greets me first thing every morning and gets me out of bed — is the unending opportunity to crank up the creative jalopy and take it for a spin.

Above all, success has given me the time to paint as I most care to, as I hoped to when I left my dead-end job in London and took my first studio in Ramatuelle, almost forty years ago.

As I longed for when stealing a little time to sketch with Ruth on a hillside in southern France.

As when heartsick and lonely in a mall on the art circuit.

As when looking in windows of upscale Soho art galleries while knocking out $100 canvasses for shady uptown dealers.

As I set my mind to when giving up everything and returning to Nantucket determined to raise myself to a new artistic level.

Transcending even the financial success and artistic appreciation, I can now look at myself in the mirror and know that my old art professor would be pleased. As would, I feel, all the teachers and advisors I have had over the years.

One works for them a bit, after all. The traditions of art were well established by the time of Leonardo. One never picks up a brush in a vacuum.

I have the chance now to savor the never-ending subtleties of art. When one has the time to explore, every brush stroke begins in mystery. There are moments when I feel that as an artist I am catalyst, a vehicle for the universal generator to make a statement through me. Call this what you will — Nature, Cosmic Intelligence, Being, or God. By any name, it is a deep well. I don't know from where or how it inexplicably descends and works through me — and I hope I never find out. I'm just grateful to be a part of it.

With success comes the responsibility, if one has a smidgen

of social conscience, to give back. To lend a hand to those weary travellers on the way up. To share the wisdom that one accumulates on the road. I subscribe to this. I do believe that one should give something back, contribute to the greater good.

One might expect that as a person grows older, he becomes wiser. Sorry to disappoint you, but I have no pearls to lay at your feet. I seem capable of making the same stupid mistakes that I made when a lad. Age does not seem to have blessed me with insightfulness. I can go ga ga over a woman with the same naivete as when I was sixteen with pimples. I still see the good in everyone and overendow regularly. I'm a soft touch and still have difficulty saying no.

It is bewildering to me how far I have come. What do you imagine the odds would have been?

Setting: outbreak of World War Two, civilization going to hell in a shit bucket, bombs falling, houses exploding.

Character: a young boy from an impoverished working-class family with an invalid father living in the grimy region of northern industrial England. Mother widowed when son just thirteen. The young lad's first job at twelve: delivering coal from before dawn till schooltime every morning.

I don't think that the odds would even have been posted. But I'm here to tell you, that it turns out that I would have been a good bet.

If I have learned anything, it is to never give up. My father once sent me outdoors to face a bully nearly twice my size. He reasoned that if I ran from him, I would keep running. After a fierce battle, I bloodied the boy's nose and had no trouble from him again.

Lesson learned, perhaps, for I have faced most of the bullies life has flung at me in much the same way: head on. Like a prizefighter always getting up, I have somehow crawled to my feet for more punishment.

Each time I rose, I instinctively moved in the direction set by the compass in my heart. I moved toward what I love, and that has made all the difference.

Success has not brought a desire to relax. I now work even harder than before. But when I take time off, I can afford to travel to places that soothe my soul; to destinations that quench

the thirst and tickle the toes. I have returned numerous times
to Ramatuelle, sketching, painting, recharging.
It has been a hell of a journey. And it's far from over.

All in all, not bad for a lad from the sooty end of northern
England!